THE POWER OF DECISION

Also by
Raymond Charles Barker

THE SCIENCE OF SUCCESSFUL LIVING

TREAT YOURSELF TO LIFE

RICHER LIVING
(*with Ernest Holmes*)

SPIRITUAL HEALING FOR TODAY

YOU ARE INVISIBLE

COLLECTED ESSAYS OF RAYMOND CHARLES BARKER

THE POWER OF DECISION

REVISED AND UPDATED EDITION

Raymond Charles Barker

The Power of Decision

Revised and Updated Edition, 1988

ISBN: 0-87516-699-7
Library of Congress Catalog Card Number: 87-32058
First DeVorss Publications Edition, 1996
Third Printing, 2002

DeVorss & Company, Publisher
P.O. Box 550
Marina del Rey, CA 90294-0550
www.devorss.com

Printed in the United States of America

Contents

Preface

TWENTY-ONE YEARS AGO I gave a series of lectures at a seminar on the subject, "The Power of Decision." Those attending found the ideas presented to be extremely helpful. So I made the decision to write this book and to give it this title.

I am certain that the principles and ideas explained in these pages will help many people to clarify their thinking and to make correct decisions. In my own life, I have proved them to be true. Too few people are living the life they really want to live. Life can be lived fully and richly. It all depends upon the decisions the person makes. Right decisions await your discovery of them. They are already in your mind. This book will help to reveal them to you.

1

The Intelligence Factor

THE INDIVIDUAL'S ABILITY to act unintelligently in a universe of Intelligence is amazing. Unintelligence functioning in human consciousness produces wrong decisions. As a result of these wrong decisions, people limit themselves with sickness, financial strain, family quarrels, and frustration, all of which are unnecessary. The power to make right decisions is yours, and this book will reveal to you methods for creating a healthy mind that will cease making erroneous decisions.

Modern science proves the universe, the cosmos, to be an arena of Intelligence wherein Intelligence, left to its own devices, will act and react intelligently. Science finds cause in creation by seeking the creative process as it functions in a framework of Intelligence known as order premised upon law. This creative process individualized in man is his capacity for right decisions.

The Infinite Mind could not act unintelligently. The cosmos would not be the visibility of total idea, law, and order if the Infinite ever knew an instant of confusion. Cause is never indecisive, never disturbed, and never defeated. It continues to act intelligently as law and order no matter what we do with our lives. Time and space forever remain the same as we move through them. Man may be limited, but the universe is not.

Intelligence Created You

Any creation of an Infinite Intelligence would have to be intelligent. Also, the purpose, the plan, and the process of coming into being would necessarily be intelligent. We are an intelligent result of an Infinite Mind acting with purpose, in ways of Intelligence, to express Itself as Intelligence in a universe of Intelligence. Law and order are as inherent in an individual as they are in the universal scheme of things.

The newborn child is the result of Intelligence. For months, the Intelligence in the mother's subconscious mind has been at work to bring this child into the world. It emerges into a world of possibility and flexibility to think and feel its way through its life span. It is equipped with Intelligence, and this Intelligence will unfold and evolve as the child is trained in intelligent ways to act and react in living. We think of the newborn child as being *cute,* but rarely as being Intelligence in action. Every child individualizes the Infinite Mind.

How Problems Are Born

The manifest universe is the continuous operation of a First Cause, which is Mind. We are also a continuous operation of this First Cause as Mind in conscious action.

Our conscious and subconscious Intelligence, acting in and on the universal subconscious of the cosmos, has total power for self-expression and self-evolution. There is one God, one Mind, one Cause, and one Intelligence, and we individualize this. Unto us is given the totality of Mind for our use and for our distribution of Its ideas into form.

Troubles result when an unintelligent factor is introduced into a field of intelligent activity. Worry is an unintelligent factor, as are fear, hate, and resentment. This list could include all the negatives known. Here is the birth of the problem. Worry is the gestation period during which a negative situation is produced by our thought and appears in our experience as a problem.

The Universal Mind, being impersonal, not knowing what It creates yet knowing how to create it, remains undisturbed by the unintelligent creations of our thought which temporarily exist within it. God is undisturbed by our wrong decisions, which are our unintelligent actions in a Universal Mind of Intelligence.

Know Yourself As Intelligence

After you read the next sentence, pause and then speak it aloud. *I am pure Intelligence, always acting intelligently.* Does your mind instinctively react with a *no*? Does this statement go against all your present self-conclusions? If it does, then you need the instruction in this book. Mind and what It creates are one. Jesus said, "I and my Father are one." (John 10:30)

You were born out of Intelligence, as Intelligence, to express Intelligence. Worry, fear, disease, argument, and frustration are not your normal heritage. These are abnormal, unhealthy uses of mind and emotion which you have wrongly assumed to be necessary to your everyday living. Your rebuttal that these negative states are normal because everyone has them does not make them so. All the sickness in the world cannot disprove health as normal. All the sorrow in the world does not prove joy to be abnormal. It is obvious that health, joy, plenty, love, and self-expression are the normal modes of living.

The fact that you and every other living soul want health, wealth, joy, and self-expression indicates that their possibilities are already in you, or you could not seek them in your world of experience. If they are within you, how did they get there? Mind individualized these potentials in your consciousness because, only as you express these needs, are you expressing life intelligently.

A New Self-Awareness

I am pure Intelligence, always acting intelligently. If you can say this without subconscious rejection of the fact, you are well along on the pathway of spiritual understanding. If the central idea involved here causes no conflict in your acceptance of yourself as Intelligence, then you are ready to live effectively. You cannot go beyond your own self-accepted image. As long as you underestimate yourself, you cannot succeed in life. No person is stupid. Stupidity is only a misuse of Intelligence in nonintelligent ways. Everyone, including you, is Mind in action, with the potentials of greatness awaiting the individual's demand that they shall come forth out of the depths of consciousness and begin creative action.

To develop this new consciousness of yourself as Intelligence, use the following spiritual treatment, both silently and audibly. It will awaken the dormant possibilities within you and start their activity.

There is one Cause, one Mind, one Source. I am, because this Cause created me out of Itself in order to express Itself as me. This Cause, being pure Mind, created me as pure Mind in action. God knows me as an intelligent vehicle of Its great ideas. Therefore, I now know myself as the Mind of God in expression. I am an alert, vital individualization of the Infinite Mind. I am Intelligence, Wisdom, and Knowledge. Every idea I need is already within my consciousness. These ideas are now activated in my thought, and I am fully aware of them. Henceforth and forevermore, I shall make right decisions.

No Self-Argument

Your human mind may refute this with the argument that you have done your best through the years, yet you have made many wrong decisions. No one has ever done his best. The greatest creative minds, producing masterpieces in art, literature, dance, music, and the sciences, have never been satisfied with their works. Never judge yourself by what you have done. Judge yourself in terms of what you will do. You are not the past. You are the present becoming the future. You are a potential of Mind and this Mind knows only the *now*. It never sits in judgment on anyone, keeps no records, and knows only the good of you.

The concert pianist may play a round of golf. The onlooker sees him as a golfer; his friends know him as a pianist. The fact that he is a golfer does not refute the fact that he is a pianist. The fact that you have made mistakes does not negate the fact that you are Intelligence in action. Every person living has made mistakes. Those who proceed with living never waste time licking their wounds. New ideas take them the next step of the way.

Separate in your thinking the golfer from the pianist. The next concert will reveal his genius at the piano. Separate yourself from your past wrong conclusions, for these are no longer what you are. You are Intelligence making right decisions, for you are directed by right ideas, ideas that are functioning in the now, this day, this hour, this minute. Life never made a problem person. It made a person capable of handling problems.

You Are Not the Problem

You are not now, nor have you ever been, the problem. You are the person who sees the problem in order to activate the idea necessary to solve the problem. Ideas, not physical bodies, solve problems. Mind and emotion are the essentials of life, and you are mind and emotion. You are never the office, the thing, or the situation. You are Intelligence, capable of knowing the right idea at the right time to make the right decision. Your right ideas, activating right decisions, sound the death knell to all negatives. Evil cannot linger on the pathway of the right-minded, up-to-date thinking individual.

"The path of the just is as the shining light, that shineth more and more unto the perfect day." (Proverbs 4:18) That scripture defines you as you really are. The universe is undisturbed by human stupidity and ignorance of what the individual really can be. The universe is never in a hurry. It is law and order. It waits for the individual to come to his senses and know himself aright. Once you know yourself as Mind, you forevermore control your experience through ideas, and not through the manipulation of material events. Thinkers change the world, and you are a thinker.

Watch Your Alibis

As a thinker, you determine your experience. There is nothing to oppose you but your own subconscious patterns of inferiority and frustration. Make mental notes of your alibis and excuses for your mistakes. These will reveal to you the patterns in your subconscious mind which need to be negated by you. The Spirit within you wants you to see yourself as you have created yourself. Seeing your own self-creation, you can then, through mental treatment, gradually whittle away your deeply rooted failure patterns and replace them with a new self-acceptance concept that will cause you to create what you want in your world.

Ernest Holmes, the founder of Religious Science, wrote, "there is no sin but a mistake, and no punishment but an inevitable consequence."* God can only do for you what you do for yourself. You may be one of those persons who thinks he cannot help being what he is. Wake up right now to a great fact of life. You and you alone are responsible for your life.

Intelligence created you and set you free on a path of self-discovery and self-decision. Your problems are unintelligence functioning in a field of Intelligence. They hurt because they are abnormal and unnecessary. Most people

* *The Science of Mind* (Dodd, Mead and Company, New York), pp. 110–111.

hug their problems to their bosoms. They place the tentacles of worry and fear around the problem so that it cannot go away. They give their whole attention to it. They think it and feel it. Then they re-think and re-feel it. These people glory in their martyrdom and believe themselves to be made virtuous because of their sufferings.

Problems Do Not Improve You

When you know the truth, you are set free from the untruth. When you know yourself as evolving, expanding Intelligence, you set yourself free from your former patterns of unintelligence. You no longer blame the world, the nation, or your family. Most certainly you do not place the blame on God. Neither do you wallow in self-pity, self-deceit, or self-depreciation. Jesus was not interested in the past causation in the mind of the man at the Pool of Bethesda. He said to him, "Arise, and take up thy bed, and walk," (Mark 2:9), and the man did just that. Instantly, the man was cleared of years of negative thinking, years of worry and defeat. It was a new man who went on his way rejoicing in his health. You can do the same thing when you reconceive yourself as Intelligence in action. Everything creative responds within your mind when you give it intelligent decision. All improvement is dependent upon you seeing yourself as being greater than you are. Then your potentials stir within you and your creative capacities unfold. By your own inner self, you are led aright, and you glimpse the *you* that you are going to be.

Cause and Effect

An unintelligent use of mind can only produce an unintelligent result. You do not blame the sun for the shadow. The sun is not causing the shadow; an object or person blocking the sun causes the shadow. The shadow is the result of an obstruction. Your problem is the result of an obstruction in your own thinking. You are not letting life flow through you in the way life really works. Divine Intelligence has never created a problem for any of its creations. Like the sun, It is forever Itself, forever giving of Itself and unaware of the misuse that we are making of this great gift. Standing with your back to the sun, you can watch your shadow; standing with your face to the sun, you see it not. Not seeing your shadow, it has no existence in your awareness. Therefore, it has no reality in your experience.

Problems are the shadows created by man when he refuses to face the light of Intelligence and therefore makes wrong decisions and abides in the halls of worry, confusion, and defeat. The problem could not exist if you did not exist to create it and experience it. Shift your attention from your concern with the problem, and give this same amount of thinking and feeling to your awareness of yourself as Intelligence in action. Then a right idea will happen in your thinking, and you will triumph over the enemies of your own preconceived wrong ideas. You are a new cause bringing forth a new effect. The new effect is one you like and one which benefits you, for it was born in Intelligence and was nurtured by your own intelligent planning.

Will It Work?

The critic says that this method of redirected mental action is too easy. He feels that a more profound system would work better. This is due to the false concept that profundity is indicative of spirituality. It is not true that the more highly we educate the intellect, the fewer problems we shall have. There would not be a problem on the face of the earth today if this were so. There are more people living now with more knowledge and more know how than ever before in the history of this planet. Our problems have not lessened. They have intensified.

The simplicity of Jesus was superseded by the complexity of Paul. The simplicity of the Nazarene was interpreted by the scholars and, in their many interpretations, the clear, correct original instruction was lost. Jesus' concept, change your thought and thereby change your experience, was lost in the theological systems guaranteeing a future heaven and a future hell. Today was lost in tomorrow. The past was hallowed and made good when so little of it was really good. The right-thinking message of Jesus is a today technique for a today world.

Yes, this teaching will work. As you introduce creative new ideas into the universal Intelligence that is Mind, you bring forth what you want, when you want it.

Have What You Want

There is nothing wrong in having what you want, provided it is moral and harms no other person. There is no virtue in self-deprivation. Western nations now state that there is no virtue in poverty. They are seeking to wipe out poverty, to give all people the ways and means to have full and creative lives. The day is past when theology can proclaim that the poor are nearer the Kingdom than the rich. The Divine Economy is premised on a Divine Equality. Each person is endowed with Intelligence to act in ways of Intelligence to bring forth his individual world of plenty and peace.

Although an idea, system, or philosophy is profound, it is not necessarily true. Nothing is true unless it works. And it has to work for you, not for someone else. Your mind, being the center and circumference of your experience, can and will create what you want, when you think and feel what you want. As long as you are thinking and feeling what you do not want, your mind will continue to create your private self-accepted hell on earth.

Reverse Your Mental Image

I am writing this book for those people who want to create their own good and not have it created for them by others; they are willing and able to accept the responsibility for their own mental actions. They refuse to dodge the alibis induced within their own consciousness. They face themselves, correct their own thought, and create their own heaven on earth. They have made the decision to be the creative centers of their own experiences. They no longer have blame or censure. They do not believe as others believe. They reverse their thinking and make certain it agrees with the goals of their decision. They hold fast to the line. They do not waiver. They know, and what they know causes their good to happen.

You can do this. You may say that you cannot, but you can. During the past fifty years of my teaching the Science of Mind, I have seen with my own eyes the improved status of hundreds of persons who faced up to themselves and corrected their mental procedures. The chronic invalid who decided to be healthy. The chronic failure who decided to be a success. The chronic lonely soul who decided to open the communications of love and let himself be loved. All kinds of troubles have been met, faced, and solved.

What about the failures? Of course there have been hundreds of failures. No Science will work unless the person applying it follows the laws of that Science. The half-hearted in any field accomplish little. Those whose enthusiasm wanes soon adjust again to their own complaints. No single medicine cures all who are ill of the same disease. Only the curable can be cured.

Unfinished Business

Creation is continuous. We exist in a continuum of creative process. Modern thinkers would like to believe that God has gone out of business. This is an impossibility. The Infinite Mind has to be an Infinite Process. Being Infinite, it cannot be limited by Its own creation. It cannot be conditioned by person, situation, or limitation. These factors are man's creation and they exist temporarily in the Infinite as does the wave on top of the sea. The sea remains itself as the wave appears and disappears. The Mind of God is eternal Cause in an eternal Process of thinking within Itself, upon Itself, creating ideas of Itself which It projects into form through the Law of Itself. The Infinite is forever in the process of Self-Discovery. This Self-Discovery, individualized in man, is called evolution. We are the Infinite unfolding Its newly discovered aspects. Into our consciousness is pouring, at every instant, a flood of new ideas born of the Spirit, the Infinite Mind. These are the living waters which, Jesus said, if we would drink therefrom, we would never thirst again. There is no more indecision when the inner fount of ideas is sought and found, praised and explored.

The Five Senses

We seek too little within ourselves for right ideas and correct answers. We accept the testimony of our five senses as being the reality of life. Yet every mystic and teacher, every religion and philosophy, have explained with care that the factual world should always be questioned. Because a thing is a fact does not mean it is a reality. The search for ideas from within your own consciousness brings satisfaction. It keeps you evolving in consciousness and unfolds the new, the fresh, and the different. It is progress.

The repetition of that which is known is not progress. What you know indicates what is still to be known. No person has ever known enough. Jesus told his followers that they would be led into all Truth and do greater works than he did. His was an awareness of the eternal evolutionary process of ideas unfolding in man, as man. The accumulation of things and the arrangement of situations leads to false security. These please the senses and lull the creative demands that arise from within. They proclaim that all is well on the surface, while underneath in the depths of man's consciousness retrogression proceeds. Consciousness must be fresh if decisions are to be right.

Nourishment for the Mind

New ideas are as essential for the mind as food and water are for the physical body. You cannot progress on the basis of the ideas that are now directing your thinking-feeling nature. You can stand where you are, amidst the demonstrations of your past causation, and watch the cracks appear in the mortar of your accumulations. You can run hither and fro to patch up the present to hold it as it is. But Life will always win out in the long run. Only new ideas, arising in consciousness from the inner fount of the Infinite Mind, will make certain your pathway in progressive revelation.

You need new ideas, new motivations, and new horizons of accomplishment. I need them as much as you do. Life has already given them to us through the unfinished business of the Infinite Mind. They await our attention. They are seeking us as open doors through which they can appear in material form. They need us as much as we need them. Use the following spiritual treatment to welcome new ideas into your awareness:

I exist in and am forever one with the Infinite Spirit, the Infinite Mind. This Mind is forever evolving new ideas of Itself, and these ideas are in my consciousness now. I am the means by which they appear. These ideas I now welcome. All subconscious opposition to them is now negated in my mind. I want, need, and have God's fresh ideas. They are my mental nourishment. They give me new directions. They lead me to right decisions.

Reject What You Do Not Want

The decision to let go of that which has completed its course in your experience is even more important than the decision to welcome new ideas. You cannot walk forward by looking backward. New wine cannot be put into old bottles, for the Bible states that the old bottles will break. You intuitively know what should depart from your life. Every once in a while, a flash in your consciousness informs you of a once-alive idea that is now dead. The human mind dislikes change and puts off until tomorrow what it should release today. Decide right now on the ideas and situations that are no longer of benefit to you. Make a list of them. These are impediments on your pathway of success. Until they are dismissed and the consequences of their release are completed, your new ideas cannot appear in mind.

The power of the word *no* is tremendous. What you mentally say *no* to will begin to depart in ways of order and in ways of peace. The failure to say *no* to completed situations eventually results in disrupting conditions that are unpleasant and unnecessary. The word *no* declared in mind eliminates all congestion. It is clear and direct to the point. The subconscious mind knows the word *no* as a law of elimination. It acts upon it to release those ideas which no longer have creative life in them. The subconscious mind, having within it all subjective Intelligence, proceeds to eliminate the idea which is cause and the effect which is the problem. It acts in intelligent and right ways to do this.

How to Do It

Try it. Take one problem that you want to solve. Make certain that you really want to be rid of it. Say aloud that you want to be rid of it, that it cannot continue in your life. Declare that this decision is final and irrevocable. Mentally picture yourself as no longer having the problem. Get the feeling that the problem is gone and shall never return. Stay in this mood for several minutes. Then change your whole trend of thinking to something creative and interesting. Think something that is pleasing to you.

The rest of the day or evening, watch your thought so that you do not interfere with the subconscious process of elimination of that old condition. Every time you begin to re-think the problem, *stop* and shift your attention to the fact that it no longer exists in your world. Never worry about it again or you will be reclaiming it, reactivating it. Always, your momentary consideration of it must be that it has gone and can never return. It is dead and buried. More than that, it has no existence in you or your affairs. Before going to sleep at night, thank the God you believe in that the problem has disappeared. The next day, keep up this creative process. Say to your subconscious mind:

My subconscious mind is a function of the Universal Mind. It obeys my word and acts upon it. I have declared the dissolution of this condition. I now reaffirm my decision. I no longer want, need, nor have this negative situation. It has gone into nothingness. It no longer has power over me. I recall it to mind no more. I am free, praise God, I am free. Indwelling Mind, you have now given me my freedom from it.

Intelligence Is Inviolate

Thank God the universe is foolproof! Many have sought out inventions to upset the cosmic order, and all they have done is to destroy their own peace of mind and comfort. Unless your thinking is premised on the Intelligence of Life Itself, you will continue in the valley of struggle and strain. You will create your problems through wrong decisions, and your frustrations will multiply. All of this is unnecessary.

There is one Mind in continuous creation, and you are a resident in It. It created you in order to act through you. It has given you the equipment you need to live effectively and with a minimum of trouble. But you have to think as the Universal Mind thinks. You have to work mentally and emotionally as It works.

There is one basic mental Law. What you place in your subconscious mind must appear as your experience. Your subconscious mind acts as a Law of Creation. Why it does this, no one knows. It is automatic and impersonal. It functions this way in every person, regardless of race, color, or creed. It is not dependent upon intellect, knowledge, reason, or wisdom. It is a Law and It is inviolate, just as the Mind which functions through It is inviolate. To the metaphysician, this Mind and this Law are the two fundamentals of living.

In other words, what you think, you think into your subconscious mind. This mind accepts your thought and acts upon it. It cannot do otherwise. It is its nature to act this way. You cannot think and feel negatively over a period of time and have positive situations maintained in your experience. The Law of the Subconscious can only bear the kind of fruit based on the seed ideas you have given it. Jesus said you could not gather figs from thistles. Paul called this sowing and reaping. The Hermetic Teaching stated that what goes in must come out. All are saying the same thing.

Decide to Control Your Life

If you decide to take control of your life and determine what will take place in your everyday living and creative planning for the future, you need the knowledge just presented. Your control depends upon your conscious awareness that your individual subconscious mind is a law of cause and effect. Nothing has ever happened to you or taken place around you that was not the result of your subconscious mind. That is a big statement, but it is true. You may mentally argue that it is not so, but eventually you will realize that it is so.

You were born as Intelligence in a universe of Intelligence to unfold, evolve, and create as Intelligence. Unfortunately, the world does not believe this. So we spend the first eighteen years of life having knowledge crammed into us. Our value to the world is based on how many facts we know. We are not considered as Intelligence; rather we are considered as humans who need to be made intelligent. As adults, we assume we are intelligent for we have diplomas to prove it.

All along this pathway, we have been pure Intelligence awaiting our self-awareness as such. Growing up, we have known ourselves as the child, the teenager, the young adult. We have been conditioned to think of ourselves as name, career, bank account, and social position. I agree that much of this is necessary, but not as necessary as we have made it.

You are greater than you think you are. You hold the key to life in your mind. You *can* act intelligently in a universe of Intelligence. You *can* decide what shall go into your subconscious mind. You *can* think what you want and thereby have your subconscious mind produce what you want. You *can* control your present experience and plan and determine your future. Thousands have done this. Other thousands are now doing this. Why not join their ranks and become what you want to be?

The Danger of Procrastination

The present moment is the time for decision. In fact, you are making decisions all the time. In the next chapter, I will show you that indecision is actually a decision. It is a decision to fail. Right now is the time to move from the level of unintelligent day-by-day drifting to the level of decisive mental action.

I have said earlier in this chapter that all problems are the result of unintelligent thinking and feeling in a field of Intelligence that must assume what you are thinking and feeling is what you really want to have as your experience. In any problem, a new train of ideas is the beginning of the cure. But the new ideas must fascinate your attention. Old ideas have a tremendous hold in your subconscious mind. They are familiar territory. They require no great mental effort to keep them activated. You rethink them with ease. You have already convinced your subconscious mind that they are valid and warrant its continued operation of them.

Such comfortable states of consciousness are hypnotic and should be avoided. It takes courage to shake off the routines of comfort and start adventuring with the control of your own life. Here is where the important role of decision comes in—the decision to stay as you are for you are at home in your present limitation, or the decision to be uncomfortable for a while and gradually enjoy new horizons of living. The Law of Mind leaves you free. Free to stay as you are and keep on patching up the present and living in a false hope that tomorrow will be better. Free also to grasp the reins of your mind and emotions and emerge from the cocoon of the usual into the wide new world of the unusual.

Ideas Are Fascinating

I assume that, having read this far, you have decided to act as Intelligence, to remove the negatives that are limiting you, and to proceed in life under the law of your own thought, in directions you choose for yourself. The metaphysician finds ideas more fascinating than things because ideas produce things. His or her interest is in controlling cause, thereby controlling effect. The practice of this Science is not sitting around daydreaming of what you want. That produces nothing but delusion. I am not teaching delusion. I am explaining how your mind is working, has always worked and will always work. Ideas detemine your life. They are cause. You are a thinker of ideas. You can select the ideas you want and proceed to think them. As you think them, your subconscious mind accepts them and produces situations like unto them. No one can do your thinking for you. You are the only thinker in your experience. The responsibility for your choice of ideas cannot be dodged. You may say that you cannot help thinking the ideas that are now fascinating your consciousness. You may say that everyone else is thinking these same ideas.

If Jesus had thought the ideas that the people of his day were thinking, we would never have had the clear instruction and proof, which he gave us, of the value of new ideas. This man did not think sickness was necessary. He was a spiritual rebel, a courageous individualization of Life. He thought what he wanted to think. He chose the ideas that would function in his consciousness. He did not conform to the world thinking around him. He stood in his own clear knowing, and this clear knowing improved the world.

Ideas are fascinating if you seek out the kind that fascinate you. Humdrum ideas need to be discarded. A new central idea that is possible, strong, and creative is needed to hang your lesser ideas upon. This fascinating idea should not be based on past experience. It is a future idea to be thought in the now. It should be one that will make you happier, healthier, more prosperous, more loving, and less frustrated. This idea is already within your mind, waiting for you to awaken to it, grasp it and think it. Not based on things which have gone before, it causes fresh and exciting new aspects to develop in your life. It invites your consideration to grow in consciousness by experiencing something new, something greater than has ever happened to you. The Infinite Mind invites you to become a new person in a new experience. Only when you are this are you fulfilling your high calling in Mind.

Unlimited Possibilities

I reaffirm my faith in the individual and his ability to determine his own experience through right decision, followed by intelligent mental-emotional action. When any individual realizes that he or she individualizes the totality of possibility, he or she is then able to be what they want to be and to have what anyone wants to have. As long as people believe themselves to be heirs to the flesh and the problems thereof, they are in bondage to old, outmoded beliefs.

Man was not born to suffer and to sin. You were born of Intelligence to soar the heights. A perfect Mind could not create out of Itself anything but Itself. As the cosmos bears witness of a pervading Intelligence, so does man when he lives on the high levels of his consciousness. These high levels are in all people and instantly available as the individual turns in thought to them. They were planted in man from the beginning of time. They are untouched by human experience. They await man's recognition of himself as the heir of Mind functioning in the unconditioned arena of time and space.

You are not an observer of the universe. You are a vital participant of the universe. Let no one ever again tell you of your unimportance. God did not make a mistake when you were born. Intelligence created you to live in these times because you are equipped to meet the challenges of these times. You are the right person, in the right place, to create a right world for yourself. All the resources of the Infinite are already yours. They need you as a means of self-expression.

You are the result of your past decisions. You will become and experience the result of your present decisions. Join me in deciding on the side of greatness.

2

Indecision

SUCCESS AND FAILURE are results of the use of mind. Every success-motivated mind has been a decisive mind. Every failure-motivated mind has been an indecisive mind. Only the dreamer who acted with decision on his dream brought forth something new and valuable. It takes as much hard mental work to fail as it does to succeed. Failure is actually a success negative. It is the result of consistent negative patterns in the subconscious mind. Worry always begets indecision.

Your only tools in life are your mind and emotions. The most successful people in all fields of activity use the same mind and the same emotions that you are using. The genius does not have more mind than you do. He consciously or subconsciously knows how to use his mind to get the results he wants. The same is true of his use of emotions. He knows what he wants to do and assumes that he can do it. This assumption is his decision.

You think and feel. How you think and feel determines your place in life. As you are the only thinker in your mind, you can decide how you will think and how you will feel. It is as simple as that. Your decision, right or wrong, gives direction to your subconscious mind, and you are on your way to your end result. Life responds to your decision by corresponding. All the ideas you need reveal themselves in right order and sequence once you have arrived at decision.

Every important event in your life has taken place because of a decision made by you or by someone else. Review some of these important times in your experience and you will note the truth of my statement. No great event happens by chance. It is caused by the decisive thinking of a person or persons. A decision alerts the subconscious energies that a sound and solid idea is being accepted by the conscious mind. Upon that acceptance, the law of consciousness acts and a new event or situation is born.

The Will to Fail

Indecision is actually the individual's decision to fail. Many people are indecisive all their lives. From the cradle to the grave, they annoy relatives, friends, and business associates with the constant question, "Tell me what I should do." Their subconscious indecision pattern is strong and clear. They seem powerless to break it. They can, but they do not know that they can. Also, they do not realize how disastrous this indecision pattern can be. Usually, this pattern is subconsciously established in the first six years of life. Parental domination or a similar home situation does not permit the child to make his own decisions. This overprotection initiates the lifelong habit of dependency upon other people to solve his problems.

Stop Asking for Advice

The chronic advice seeker is a sorry soul. The inability to accept the responsibility of running your own mind may well be the major sin of life. It is a pattern that can be broken. I have known many people who have done this. Not easily, but with wise counseling, they saw themselves in a new light. They accepted the first principle of individuality, which is self-determination.

Freedom of mind action is your birthright. It remains your latent potential if you are an indecisive person. It can always be activated. You were born to be you. Your consciousness is fully equipped to express you. But you have to realize that you can be you. Otherwise, you are a potpourri of other people's decisions. You are a second-place person getting from life a small portion of the good that is possible. Leaning on the consciousness of others, you are not being what you can be. Eating three meals a day in restaurants will never make you a cook. Not until you enter your own kitchen and use its equipment can you start to cook. The first results may not be very inspiring, but at least you are now cooking.

All intelligence abides in your consciousness and awaits your call upon it. You may say you do not know what to do. But at the center of your mind is the clear decision you should make. It is right there. It can be found instantly when your mind turns to it. "Seek, and ye shall find." (Matthew 7:7)

The Answer Is Within

The world of other people's decisions is not your world. No matter how wise and kind these people may be. No matter how much they love you and care for you. They are only maintaining your childhood pattern of indecision, the pattern of leaning on other minds rather than on your own. God made your mind for you to think *your* thoughts and not someone else's thoughts.

Why this apparent need for you to make your own decisions? You seek your own success and this success comes when you use your own resources. Every successful person is a success because he used ideas that arose within his own mind. Original thinking does not come from another person. It happens in your own mind. Fine ideas can be transmitted to you from others, but originality awaits your own self-discovery. It is already in your consciousness, planted there from the beginning. You are spiritually equipped to be an original thinker. Declare that you are and interesting ideas will come to your mind. These will not fit your usual patterns of thinking. They will make you uncomfortable. But do not reject them. They beckon you to areas of new successes. They invite you to be a prospector of gold mines of new events. You glimpse the maturity of self-knowing, and you leave the immaturity of seeking help.

The Universe Is Decisive

The originating Mind of the cosmos knows what It is doing, and It does Its work well. It has a mathematical accuracy of law and order. It cannot have any self-argument, and It is never indecisive. It asks no questions. It leans on no one. It proceeds in Its business of creating the new, the better, and the different. It cannot stagnate nor can It be defeated. All is in order in the universe. You may call a hurricane disorder, but the meteorologists know it as order. They are aware of its beginning, its course, and its ultimate end. They chart it accurately and well. To them, it is an orderly phenomenon as cause, process, and conclusion.

You exist in and are a part of this originating universal Mind. All of Its law and order is instantly available to you. In fact, this Mind is already in your consciousness awaiting your awareness of It. You are never apart from It. You may unconsciously isolate yourself from It, but It cannot isolate Itself from you. It *is* and you *are* that which It *is*. There is but one Mind, and you are a thinker in It. All of Its ideas are your ideas. Its forward proceeding action of constant creation and the maintenance of that which It has created are right now functioning in your mind. The following spiritual treatment will aid you in being aware of It and thereby receiving benefits from It.

There is one originating Intelligence, Mind, and Spirit, and I am Its action, Its outlet, and Its process of revealing Itself. It knows me as Itself, and I know myself as It. Therefore, I am never indecisive. I always have the right idea at the right time. Infinite Intelligence in me knows what to do, and this knowledge is mine at every instant. Original thinking pervades my consciousness, and I am correctly decisive regarding all matters. I know what I need to know at the instant I need to know it. The results of this correct knowing of original ideas bring forth new and improved situations in my life. For this I am glad.

Let There Be

The Bible opens with the allegorical description of many decisions on the part of the Causative Mind. I suggest that you read again the first chapter of Genesis. There is not a single sentence of hesitation in it. It is clear and direct. The writer is telling, by means of an ancient poetical form, a concept of the way the Infinite Mind creates out of Itself. It does this by first forming clear, definite ideas of that which It wants as form. It next declares these ideas into form by stating, "Let there be," and the form appears. This Creative Mind is all in all. It has no one to whom It can turn for advice. It knows within Itself what It wants and proceeds to bring it to fruition. It wastes neither time nor energy. It decides and acts upon Its decisions.

This cosmic originating process is not an ancient one used only once. It is the correct way of thinking both universally and individually. What God does on the grand scale of the cosmos you can do on the plane of the particular. In fact, the only success process is this process. Few successful people ever realize that they are using a spiritual means to achieve their goals, but they are. They would shout *no* if you told them this, but the truth remains that there is only one success process. Know what you want, decide it shall happen, and act upon the decision. Your conscious mind makes the decision and your subconscious mind acts upon the decision.

Give It to Your Subconscious

In your subconscious mind is the creative process of the ages, the process which every successful person has used. It cannot refuse to service you. It has no favorites, and it knows no limitations. It awaits your demand that it act. Upon your demand, it proceeds to fulfill this demand without stress or strain. The mental machinery of your subconscious mind moves into action in orderly ways and draws upon resources far greater than the conscious mind could ever know. No wonder that modern metaphysicians call this function of mind *God*. They sense the magnitude of its ability and they use this tremendous creative potential to produce what they want in life.

All of this is already in you. The great use it. The non-great do not, so they remain the non-great. Decide upon some thing, situation, or condition that you want right now in your present life. Be definite in this decision. Do not limit your decision by investigating the probable reasons why it will never happen. That is the detour to nothing. All false speculations of defeat have to be ruled out of your consciousness. If they enter into the decision for even a fleeting moment, the decision is robbed of authority and the subconscious mind cannot act upon it. You do not need to know how the final result will come to pass. That is the function of the subconscious. It has ways and means that, if they were known, would stagger the intellect. Say to your subconscious,

"This is my decision. I now authorize you to accomplish this. I have total confidence in your abilities and resources. I authorize

this without any reservations. I do not place this demand in a framework of time or condition. It is a free demand now established in my subconscious mind. This mind now has it clearly."

Then relax and let your subconscious have free reign. Keep clear of all doubt. Keep clear of all worry. God, in your subconscious as your subconscious, is the power and the mind that accomplishes your desire. Let God be God, and keep your hands off the process.

Your subconscious will reveal to your conscious mind directions to take and ways to proceed. Idea will follow idea in perfect order and sequence. You become the observer of the creative process now taking place in you. From the observation point in the conscious mind, you watch what you wanted to have happen, happen. You are under no strain. You are the observer and the participant.

Adult or Child?

To be an effective adult requires you to make decisions. If you are not going to make decisions and continue to falter through life, then you had better accept yourself as infantile. Face it and admit it to yourself. The height of your body or the date on your birth certificate have nothing to do with your mind and emotions. Paul wrote, "When I was a child, I spake as a child, I understood as a child, I thought as a child: but when I became a man, I put away childish things." (1 Corinthians 13:11) He had accepted himself as an adult. His decisions were many, and they were one of the primary sources for the spread of the ideas of Jesus.

If you have trouble making up your mind because you are afraid of making a mistake, then you are still the immature child. Children are afraid of making mistakes because of their strong emotional need to please their parents. The adult who is indecisive is a person who is still subconsciously afraid that what he or she may do will not please some past symbol in his mind. Too often, the past still rules the present. Usually it is so camouflaged in the subconscious that the individual is completely unaware of it.

I often ask myself this: "Will my decisions today be based on today's experiences guided by the wisdom of the past, or will they be determined only by past memory patterns?" If the latter, I will make erroneous conclusions. You have to be a *today person* in a *today experience* to have the fullness of life in the here and the now. The mature adult is usually able to do this. The immature adult continues in the valley of questions, doubts and worries. His day lacks lustre, his hours have no fascination in them, and he wearies in his supposed well-doing. His problems absorb his attention, their emotional importance expands, and he is most unhappy in his home, his job, and his social relationships. So he becomes an advice seeker, hoping that his fellowman can deconfuse his confusion.

This person needs to make a decision of his own. It may be a wrong one, but all of us make wrong decisions. The mature mind accepts the result of his error and minimizes any self-guilt. He proceeds on his course and makes more decisions, the majority of them being right ones. But, when the adult who unconsciously goes back to his childhood for parental approval makes a wrong decision, he loads himself with more guilt and remorse. He accepts himself as a probable failure. He distrusts his own abilities. He is a very unhappy person.

Check your guilt load and begin rationalizing it away.

No one ever makes a mistake on purpose. Mistakes are not consciously planned. They may be subconsciously planned, but even these can be freed of their emotional importance. The lower your guilt load, the greater your mental health. You may ask if all guilt can be consciously known. No. But all your guilt does not need to be known. Years of psychological analysis might be necessary for you to become aware of only ninety per cent of your guilts. Only the guilt that is preventing you from being a whole present person needs to be known. Once you are alert to this fact, your intuition will gradually show you the areas where you need to do some rationalizing.

No power anywhere sits in judgment on you. The universe is unconcerned with your mistakes. You are your only judge, and the faculties of your mind are your only jury. Realizing that you did not err with deliberate attempt or purpose will often clear the guilt. Each guilt recognized, rationalized, and emotionally released of power will assist you to decide rightly. The following spiritual treatment will help to release your guilt.

There is one Mind, one life, one Spirit, and I individualize It. This Mind, Life, and Spirit is always thinking of me in terms of Itself. It never sits in judgment, and It has no condemnation. The goodness of life is the goodness of God. I now release all emotional power from any and all guilt in my subconscious mind. I am set free of all self-judgment and self-condemnation. I know myself as God knows me. I am free of all past errors. I am free to move forward in life. Now I make right decisions. God honors my thought and acts upon it. I prosper in all my affairs. I am free.

The Universe Is All Right

The universe is a success. It has never been defeated and never will be. Some wit has said that the only mistake God ever made was to invent man. You and I know this is not so, but many times I have wondered about it. The universe that the scientist studies is a success. The cosmic order is a magnificent display of an infinite Intelligence thinking mathematically. Unconditioned by time or space, the cosmos continues its successful action. Though man can destroy himself, the cosmos remains untouched by his destruction. A raging forest fire on a mountainside can destroy a thousand trees. Five years later, you will find small trees, self-seeded, coming up on that barren location. Ten years later, a new forest is well under way. The Creative Process cannot be defeated. It will always win out.

Self-defeat is easy to accomplish. Indecisiveness has a great deal to do with self-defeat. The man God made is intended to succeed. He is mentally and emotionally equipped to do so. It is too easy to blame the first six years of life for all our later problems. A right decision concerning the present and the future may be all that is needed to turn a failure-prone person into a success-adventuring person.

Often I have watched a party of four people seated in a restaurant reading menus. They seem to have quite a time deciding on the main course. One of them will turn to another and ask, "What are you going to have?" The friend replies that he is going to have the roast beef. At once, the questioner puts down his menu and says, "I'll have that too," thereby avoiding his own decision. This may seem like a trivial illustration, but it is not. It reveals how easy it is to fall into the habit of having other people decide matters for us. Such a person has, without realizing it, lessened his individuality.

A woman in her forties came to me for counseling several years ago. Her problem was indecision. She was unable to walk into a store and select her own clothes. For over twenty-five years, she had tried, but, as she said, "I only waste the sales girls' time." Her husband had to do all the shopping for her clothes. Instantly I knew what was the matter. I said to her, "Since you were a small child, you were never allowed to pick out your own clothes. You had a domineering mother who wouldn't let you decide on anything." Her face lighted up and she said, "How did you know that?" I continued by saying, "So you made your husband into your mother." This she did not like, but she did see the point. After several sessions of counseling, she was able to break this pattern and is now able to do her own shopping. The adjustment in her subconscious mind was not an easy one, but she finally made it.

Individuality Necessitates Responsibility

Individuality necessitates decision. Individuality means that you have to be you. No matter how much people may love you, they cannot be that which you are. The Spirit individualizes Itself in every person. The inability to make decisions indicates that you have not accepted yourself as an independent individual. Many people never accomplish this self-acceptance. They lean on others all their lives. These are chronic failure people. They have not accepted the responsibility of being. They have dodged the very reason for their existence to be that which they are and not to be an accumulation of other people's opinions.

The major difference between mankind and the animal kingdom is free will or volition. Man is able to think, choose, and decide. He is only partially directed by instinct. The indecision pattern is an unconscious abrogation of individuality. It is turning your mind over to others when the purpose of your mind is for your own self-government. It is your mind. It is the gift of God in you. It contains the potentials of a full life and an expanding experience. Herein is your uniqueness, your individuality, your ability to be you—the you that you can be.

The chronic failure person does not realize what he is doing to himself. He is unaware of self-causation. He has built a subconscious alibi mechanism to explain himself to himself. He is the man who thinks he never got any breaks in life. The firm he works for does not appreciate him and promotes other men to better jobs while he stays in the same routine work year after year. Or, he may be another man who cannot hold on to jobs. His reasons are equally exterior to himself. Only through the repetitious rehearsals of their alibis can these people manage to live with some peace of mind. Always their difficulties are outside of themselves; things, situations, and events happen to them, so they think.

But situations, events, and things do not just happen to anyone. They are caused by the individual experiencing them. "For as he thinketh in his heart, so is he." (Proverbs 23:7) Modern psychology has proven the validity of this Bible statement. You project yourself on the screen of life. You are the cause to your own experience. Situations, events, and things proceed from your consciousness to appear on the screen of life. The screen of life is as impersonal as the motion picture screen in a theatre. One week a tragedy may appear on the screen and the next week a comedy may be shown. The screen does not know what it is showing to the audience. It only knows how to show it. A motion picture scene wherein a man is shot puts no hole in the screen. It remains what it is.

In your own life, you are the projector of your consciousness on the screen of experience. A child may bump his head on a door and kick the door, seeming to place blame on it. An adult does not do this. He knows that it was not the door's fault. Something in his thinking caused him to bump his head on the door. The failure-prone person needs to accept the responsibilities of life, to stop blaming the world, and to seek within himself for negative causation. "Why did this happen to me?" is usually unanswerable. "Why did I cause this to happen?" usually leads to an understanding of the cause of the problem. Every mystic, saviour and saint has told his followers that the inside of man is the explanation of the outside of man. These wise minds had found a truth and were explaining the truth they had found. They knew with intuitive certainty that it was truth. The inside of the individual is the explanation of the outside of the individual. All spiritual disciplines were to put the inside man in order and give him right directions. Right ideas arise in our consciousness. If decided upon and acted upon, they bring forth right results. Right ideas in our consciousness ignored become wrong ideas and bring forth incorrect decisions with unpleasant results.

The outside man senses effects and usually believes them. His sight, hearing, smell, taste, and touch confirm his correct conclusions. He explains himself to himself by the material facts he observes. Metaphysicians and psychologists do what the great spiritual thinkers did. They know that the interior world of mind is true cause and the external world of affairs is an effect world. External facts betray internal ideas, moods, feelings, and motivations. Paul wrote, "Be not conformed to this world." (Romans 12:2) Jesus said, "Ye are of this world; I am not of this world." (John 8:23) These are but two of many such statements by great thinkers.

This does not mean a withdrawal from the world of facts. It most certainly does not mean to deny its existence. The outside world is wonderful when you are not fooled by it. When you really know that your inside world is cause to your outside world and that you have full control over your consciousness of cause, you have true freedom of both thought and action. You think what you want and you want what you think. The world conforms to original thinkers. They never conform to it. The material world rearranges itself to accommodate what a Thinker wants, and it does so as a Thinker is thinking and deciding. There is no delay. The subconscious law of mind knows no procrastination. It acts instantly on all conscious mind decisions.

There is so much greatness to be known, thought, and experienced that I am amazed everyone is not seeking it and experiencing the great good which automatically accompanies such sound contemplation. The Psalmist wrote, "This is the day which the Lord hath made; we will rejoice and be glad in it." (Psalms 118:24) For those who can reach out to great ideas and contemplate them as being so and decide that they shall be so, the experiencing of an abundant livingness is theirs. These people cannot be defeated. There is no interior causation to cause external defeat. Certainly they use the facts which their five senses reveal to them, but they see a larger idea than the one reported by the senses. They are working in a wider arena of mental action, an arena which sees beyond sight. It knows beyond facts. It expects beyond the usual limitations. Such men and women are a joy to God and a great blessing to their fellowman. They keep the light of Truth alive and let It shine through an ever-expanding field of creative accomplishments.

The Light of the Mind

"That was the true Light, which lighteth every man that cometh into the world." (John 1:9) This statement implies that you have this Light. You can reach out for the greatness I have mentioned by reaching within your own mind to find the generic ideas placed there by the Infinite Mind. They are already yours. You need not supplicate a deity to have them. You need not fast to know them. No single church can give them to you. They are universal, impersonal, and instantly available. They are the Light of your life. They are the answer to your every need. They have the capacity to fulfill your every good desire. Ideas, not facts, are the hope of your world, and these ideas are already resident in your present mind.

The way out of trouble is a way into the mind. It is not a way of facts. It is a way of ideas. Every idea you need is instantly available at the moment you need it. The Infinite has never deserted anyone. Supply has always preceded demand. The revelation of new ideas is a constant mental process in which your mind is forever immersed. These ideas are your property by right of your being you. This is the "inheritance incorruptible" mentioned in the Bible

(1 Peter 1:4) It is not merely the property of the good. It indwells saint and sinner alike, but the saints are those wise enough to sense it and draw from it. You can join the ranks of the wise by contemplating yourself as cause. Such contemplation causes your next right idea to appear in your consciousness. Decision upon this right idea guarantees its execution in the material world by means of the law of the subconscious mind.

We would be living in a grand Utopia today if every great idea that arose in men's minds had been followed by decision and right action. Too many great ideas have been meditated upon and then discarded. Usually the thinker discards them for what seem to him to be plausible reasons. No great discovery in history has been based on plausible reasons. Automobiles were implausible in 1900. Radios were implausible in 1910. Transatlantic planes were implausible in 1920. Yet thinkers let such ideas arise in their consciousness out of the wellspring of the Infinite Intelligence. We should all be grateful that these thinkers decided to try the ideas they had. Every scientific mind has made the implausible plausible.

You Are Cause

You are cause because you can think. The only creative process there has ever been, is now, or evermore shall be is thinking. You can let new ideas happen in your consciousness as easily as you can do any of the routine things in your daily life. New ideas happen to the people who want them to happen in their consciousness. They do not happen in the minds of people who are content with themselves as they are. They do not happen in the minds of those who worship the past. The Infinite Intelligence seeks to release Itself in original ways in every man, woman and child. It has no favorites and seeks no favors. All It requires is for the person to be interested in new ideas and to be willing to act upon them through right decision. You can be that person. Even as you read this page, a new idea can dawn in your consciousness.

The Infinite Mind can only give you an idea. It has nothing else to impart to you, Its beloved consciousness. If you need things, It gives you the ideas to cause the things to manifest for you. The Infinite is the Thinker, leaving man to be the Producer. This man is you. You are the means by which the Infinite acts upon the plane of the particular. In you, through you, and as you, the Creative Process seeks outlet. You can never be what you were intended to be until you welcome this Process and reach out for the unlimited possibilities It offers to you. You were created to think, feel, decide, and act upon the decisions.

Original Ideas

Original ideas are the result of an immaculate conception. They are not from material sources. They do not arise out of past experiences. They are born in the Infinite Mind and are reborn in your consciousness without the aid of any other person. They just happen in you when you have consciously or subconsciously prepared the consciousness in which they could happen. These ideas are completely pure. As yet, they have not been adulterated by doubt or material speculation as to how, why, or when. The person who can recognize their purity and watch his thought to maintain this purity can then arrive at an acceptance of them, decide upon them, and experience their extension into the world of form.

I will never know how many original ideas that entered my mind were adulterated by my doubts. The world thinking has taught us to be wary of new ideas. It says to us that the better course is to wait and see. Many a great experience has been lost because we listened to the opinions of the masses. Yet the opinions of the masses have never caused progress. Progress happens when leaders arise with new ideas. These men and women are undaunted by material beliefs and material situations. They maintain the purity of the new idea and proceed with their decisions about it. They know that what they know is right, so their subconscious minds are able to project the new ideas into their experience. Every benefit to man has come through just this process of the aware mind, undisturbed by material reasonings, proceeding to express an idea that arose within itself.

Ideas exist in a timeless, spaceless continuum. Total potential is in their make-up. They have nothing in them to limit their full expression. They come to your mind, which is time-space conditioned. There they are put in a framework of past, present, and future. This is where mental adulteration starts. The idea is a *now* conception. Held in mind as a *now* conception, its potentials can be used, exploited and enjoyed. Too often they are weighed in the balances of the past and the future and their essence is lost.

Can you think of yourself as a timeless, spaceless continuum? If you can, you have a very expanded consciousness. You are a rarity. Average people are absorbed in a time-space consciousness. Their preoccupation about their age is evidence of this. They are either too young or too old. They dread the term *middle-aged.* They do everything possible to resist the aging process. They have been told by their churches that they will live after death, but they do not believe it, even on Easter Sunday morning. The idea of death frightens them.

You are a timeless, spaceless individualization of life. You function in a time-space arena and are usually fooled by it. Without realizing your infinity and eternity, you take original ideas and place them in limits. You hope they are so, rather than knowing they are so. Every idea in your consciousness has possibilities that can be explored. Old ideas seen from a new angle reveal new possibilities. A thousand clergymen on a Sunday morning can use the same Bible text; perhaps a hundred and fifty different denominations with creeds opposed to one another, but the same text is used to support the sermon. Through this wide spectrum of varying beliefs, each clergyman will find an original idea to expound. Here is one idea, and an old idea at that, still giving evidence of originality when functioning in varying minds.

Ideas never get stale, but people do. Ideas are eternal and their possibilities are infinite. You place upon them your own subconscious time-space limitations. The more you can envision yourself as a spiritual creation, the designed projection of the Infinite Mind, the less limits you place upon ideas and the more you leave them free to bring forth new experiences. I cannot stress too much the need for you to reconceive yourself as a continuous process of life throughout eternity. You, as individuality, did not suddenly appear on a certain day to be nothing on another certain day. You have been, are now, and shall always be you. Arise from the human mind delusion of birth certificates and death certificates and walk free from the horrendous conclusions they have evoked in your consciousness. Then, immaculate ideas will find a welcome in your consciousness, for they know you will accept them and have fuller expansion of living by means of them. They are food to the mind and substance to the emotions.

The Mind of God is a well that never runs dry. All of Its ideas are instantly available to you. Idea follows idea as day follows night. Ideas seek you out. They need you for their own self-expression. Your use of them guarantees your full self-expression. Think of your mind as the birthplace of God's intentions. Think of its grandeur, its magnificence, its magnitude. Your mind is a center of Divine activity. Forget the speculations of neurosis, inferiority complex, and negative patterns. See your mind from the higher side of life. Know your mind as the Infinite knows it. It is a place of birth, not of death. You are the deciding factor in your consciousness; therefore, in your entire world of experience. Know yourself as God knows you. God loves you because God loves Itself.

3

Decision

DECISION IS THE most important function of the individual mind. No creative process can begin until a decision is made. I could not write this chapter until I had arrived at the decision to do it. I am writing this on a lazy summer day when the outdoors invites me to many pleasant things. I have been sorely tempted to move from my typewriter and relax with friends. But I have decided that this chapter shall be written, and it shall be written now.

Having made the decision, every right idea will flow into my consciousness. Each idea will reveal itself at the instant I need it. The writing proceeds, but it could not proceed without my having decided. The creative process awaits your decision and your calm acceptance of the necessary work on your part following the decision. Idea follows idea as you proceed in the work of bringing to pass that which you decided would now be.

You are able to accomplish anything you really want to accomplish. The Infinite is yours to explore and the Infinite is never dull, stale, or commonplace. To say you do not know what to do, or you do not know what you want, is to negate the Infinite Intelligence which is individualized in you. What you are really saying is that you are too lazy to determine your own experience, or you think another person is better equipped to determine your good.

No one else on earth is better equipped to determine your good than you are. The universe has no favorites and God knows no special person. Others may have more factual knowledge and more experience. They have this because of their own decisions. Consciously or subconsciously, they decided to think new ideas, read new sources of ideas, and execute definite plans based on the new ideas they had assimilated. They know more because they decided to know more. You can do likewise.

Explore ideas as the mariners of old explored the seven seas. They were impelled by an inner fascination with that which was unknown but could be known. They risked great physical dangers and underwent great deprivations. These you will not need to face. Your decision to explore new realms of mind will not take you away from your comforts of each day unless you let your comforts coddle you into only existing rather than actually being. You were created to be. And to be, you have to emerge from the cocoon of complacency and dare to venture in consciousness across uncharted seas of mind.

Even as you read this book, there are people everywhere who have decided to expand their lives. They have decided to be well and not sick. They have decided to prosper and not continue in financial limitation. They have decided to give and receive love. They have decided to be themselves. As a result, they have right ideas revealing themselves in their minds to accomplish their decisions.

These people are willing to be temporarily uncomfortable in order to achieve expanded consciousness and reach new goals.

Such people make contributions to the world. They do not wait for others to create the new, the vital, and the futurative. They do it. They are willing to change consciousness. They consciously or unconsciously realize that they are important to the grand scheme of Life. They may never acquire fame or fortune, but they have the sense of well-being which accompanies all creative activity. You belong in their ranks.

The Invisible You

The real *you* is not only invisible, it is also immeasurable. In my class instruction in the Science of Mind, I use the following illustration to make the students realize that they inhabit a larger arena than that which the five senses reveal. I ask the reader to try this experiment. Close your eyes and take a moment to relax your body as completely as you can. Place your feet flat on the floor. Sit in a comfortable position. Let your hands relax, and be at peace. Think of yourself as being unlimited, spaceless. You are aware of your body wherever your clothes bind you, or the chair makes itself aware, or the floor beneath your shoes seems certain. Think of your forehead, your nose, your ears, the backs of your hands. Can you tell where the skin is and space begins?

Note the sides of your face and see if you can sense where the skin is. Where is the bottom of your chin? In this relaxed position, it is almost impossible to define yourself as body, meaning outline and limitation. You realize that you are not just body, you are consciousness, you are idea. You seem to extend into infinity, and you really do. You glimpse that you are an activity of thought and feeling moving through and participating in a continuum of Mind.

As you practice this simple exercise, you lessen the hold of the body consciousness that has been engrained in you by experience. You sense what the Ancients called the invisible and eternal self. That which you really are because you have always been it. This correct self-awareness is unconditioned by time or space. It knows no limitation. It only knows expansion, the unfolding of consciousness unrestricted by past experience. It has not mortgaged its future. It trusts in the Infinite Intelligence and Its ceaseless activity of ideas.

You may say that this is interesting but not practical. But it is practical. Every improvement in the lot of mankind has come about because someone expanded his consciousness. Some individual saw beyond the limitations of the *now* as known in time to the *now* as known in eternity. Some man or woman saw that that which would be already was. As idea, it was present. Therefore, as form it could become present. This is true thinking. This is creative consciousness and it can be yours.

You Are Consciousness

To say *I am consciousness* is to state what you are as individuality. It is self-definition in the timeless, spaceless sense. It has neither name nor number. It needs neither location nor means. It is completeness. It includes all process but is not process. It is pure being. It opens the trap doors to infinity and eternity. It knows no dimensions and does not need them. It operates by means of them, but is never conditioned by them. It is the *you* that you are. It is not the you that your educated consciousness has taught you as being. It is what you are in God.

This pure self-awareness is not intrigued by past, present, and future. It is aware of these lines of demarcation only as measurement, never as fact or limitation. This is not a self-concept. It is a glimpse and a sense of that Concept which you are in the larger Mind of the Infinite. It is the infinite and immeasurable you. Suddenly you are all in all. You are in all, through all, as all. In this understanding, the word *impossible* is unknown, for all knowledge and all process is yours. Whatever needs to be done is done in consciousness, for here alone is cause. Cause cannot be conditioned by effect, for cause is law unto effect. Consciousness is. All else is secondary to it. It is Spirit, and it is Truth.

As unconditioned consciousness, you are Spirit and you are Truth. To know this is the most valuable idea that can ever be known. Every spiritual system was founded by one who knew this and groped his or her way toward it. We are still doing this today. We still sense the magnitude of true consciousness only in part. We sense it, and this the materialist does not. He is so busy with his world of effects and his manipulation of them that he cannot lift his sights to a larger horizon. If he were to read this far in this book, he would cast it aside and pronounce it to be impractical metaphysical rubbish.

I know hundreds of people who have proven this larger

I am consciousness concept to be the turning point in their lives. It reversed their whole basis of making decisions. They ceased their worship of the past. They ceased their fear of the future. They cancelled out all fear of death. They decided to be cause to their world because they now realized that they were their world. They were no longer people experiencing life. They were Life experiencing itself. They were their own saviours and their own saints. They needed no messiahs. Knowing themselves in God, as God, they placed no lesser gods before themselves.

Not so the materialist. He needs his other gods. He needs another to show him the way, to promise him salvation. He needs a heaven and a hell to frighten him into behaving with sense. He needs to believe that Someone else is greater than he is. He needs another person's model, pattern, and plan.

I am consciousness frees you from all this. It causes you to emerge into the larger consciousness wherein you are the All, and the All is what you are. You are willing to be your own heaven and your own hell. You know you are your only redeemer out of the old into the new. You seek not heaven by another man's route. You are the heaven you seek and you awaken unto it, realizing your eternal experience in it. It has never left you, but you have closed your eyes to it. Now your eyes of perception are open, and that which you never left is seen. At night when you sleep, you dream the dream. In the morning, you awaken to the bed and the bedroom you never left. The dream may have been pleasant or horrendous, but you never left the bedroom nor the bed.

You Are Measureless

The whole world of facts shouts at you what you cannot do. It says that you are a victim of the times. It measures you in words of success and failure, health and disease, friends and enemies. It is emphatic about your age, your life expectancy, and finances. It affirms you as body, bank account, and ultimate death.

I am consciousness reverses all this. You know this is not so. You know yourself as pure awareness beyond the limits of time, space, and measurement, yet functioning in these arenas with ease and fulfillment. Ideas create facts, and you are now idea-minded. Intuition gives you the idea. You think the idea. The thought you think causes subjectivity to create the fact. No fact can appear in your experience unless you have accepted the idea and thought the thought. Knowing this, you order your experience and live in its freedom. You do not measure yourself with the measurements of fact and intellect. You see yourself as a becoming process, as that which yet shall be. In the Infinite, there is no measurement for there are no comparisons. The Infinite is your existence, and you encompass its potentials.

Think back to the exercise I suggested to you at the beginning of this chapter. Again shut your eyes, relax, and seek to determine where the skin on the sides of your face is. Note that you actually cannot measure the place where skin ceases and space begins. You cannot decide, for there is no decision to make. There is only the question to be contemplated and the truth to be observed. For the moment, you cannot measure this fact about yourself. Here is a place where you are measureless. Your consciousness is beyond measure. You can measure facts by taking examinations. Examinations have never proven what the individual knew on any given subject. The very word *examination* invokes a fear which negates it as a valuable tool.

At the center of your consciousness is a purpose, but not a plan. The purpose is that of the Infinite Mind aware of Itself, thereby having consciousness. This consciousness is the purpose of your being. It is why you are what you are as consciousness. It has nothing to do with what you are at the fact level. This you have self-determined and experienced. Your real purpose is you as consciousness intuitively directed by ideas, free to move in consciousness, as consciousness, experiencing endless fields of consciousness. When you decide that this is what you really are, the purpose is known to you and you perceive yourself as a continuum of thought and feeling directing your experience world with volition. You plan your own plan, for there is no one to plan it for you. You select the ideas for your own experience, for besides you as the selector, there is none other.

Trap Doors in the Mind

Intuition has too long been used at the material level only. People claim that their intuition helped them to select the right horse at the racetrack, or the right marriage partner, or the right stock to buy. If these selections turn out all right, then they are claimed to be the results of intuition. If they turn out wrongly, they are considered the results of bad judgment.

True intuition does not deal with *getting*. It deals with self-awareness. It is not the Infinite seeking to give you more things. Most of the readers of this book do not need more things. They need a larger sense of self. They need to know what they are as pure consciousness. Only then can they make correct decisions, based not on facts, things, or good judgment. These are for those who are not yet able to see that consciousness is reality, and that we move as consciousness, through consciousness, exploring consciousness, and thereby experiencing consciousness. This is not negating the material world. It is seeing the material world as consciousness temporarily locked up in form, but never limited to the form in which it is functioning.

There is a trap door in your mind. When you open it by knowing yourself as *I am consciousness,* new perceptions enter your arena of thinking. They are not perceptions of yourself as you are. They will not lead you to greater outer accomplishments, though these will automatically follow. They will lead you to a higher level of knowing where ideas are factual and things are not. Intuition is the process of self-awakening. It gives you glimpses of a larger life, a greater mind, and a deeper reason for being. We have lived too long in the belief of existing as well as we can, physically and comfortably, until death doth us part. Intuition has nothing to do with this that I have mentioned. It is God in man, as man, knowing Itself as God, not knowing Itself as man.

Intuition reveals what you always have been. Its revelations seem new and strange. I sometimes call this instruction the Science of Remembering. It is a way of recall. It is knowing what always has been, is now, and always shall be. Intuition reveals concepts that were before a physical universe began. To us, they seem new and startling because we are so sure of the physical now and uncertain of the physical future that we cannot accept consciousness as continuity. To us, the past is the past, the present is the present, and the future is the future. In pure consciousness, such delineations are nonexistent. They have no meaning; in fact they do not exist. You are, you have been, and you will be. The mystic trusts the process and proceeds in his unfoldment of consciousness without fear. He has faith in the creative process of mind.

Intuition will not make you rich or happier. It will not bring you health if you are sick. That is not its function. It will lead you into yourself for an exploration of yourself from a higher viewpoint. It is a great givingness of conceptions. It cannot be wheedled, cajoled, or threatened. It never functions under tension. Its atmosphere is peace and self-acceptance. Its purpose is not to make you a better person, nor to save your soul, nor to redeem your sins. Such theological assumptions have nothing to do with this instruction. Intuition is the process by which you become aware of yourself not as self, but as the allness and the fullness of Being.

Play your *hunches* if you wish. Often they lead to right results. They are usually a subconscious knowing which reveals itself to the conscious mind. But intuition is not this. Psychology states that what you are is the result of what you have been, and that this usually determines what you will be. This instruction does not negate this. It is true for the person who is living the usual life and not interested in much else than success, health, and happiness. At that level, the psychologists are correct. But intuition is another thing. It deals with the total man, not the man of parts divided into past, present, and future. The Infinite, being all, is not divisible. You as the consciousness of the Infinite are seeking to know yourself not as divisibility but as unity. The whole person leaves aside the person to see himself as the All. Such intuitive perception is not only for the mystics and sages. It is for you as well. It leads to total freedom from struggle, strain, and fear. It is wonderful.

Stop Defining the Future

To utter finalities regarding the future is nonsense. Evolution with its steadfast unfoldment, its law and order, will take place no matter what your peculiar opinions may be. The Infinite is not going out of business, no matter what the mind of man concludes, prophesies, or speculates. It will continue to be Itself. A question that is asked of me several times a week is, "Do you believe in life after death?" Of course I do. Knowing myself as consciousness, I have ceased to know myself as merely body and sensation. What dies? Certainly it cannot be consciousness that dies, for consciousness is independent of the body, even when it is using body. Dreams are independent of body. They have no conscious connection with it.

The future is an unfoldment of consciousness, an unfoldment of ideas, revealing to me what I really am. This consciousness has its own means of functioning on all planes. The Intelligence that produced my present body will take care of me when I leave it. It knows how to fulfill me as Its consciousness through all time and in all space. Being will keep right on being. I exist in this Being, as this Being. Being an individualization of It now, I shall never be less. I can only be more of It for the trap door of intuition will never close, and I shall always be more aware of myself as consciousness. Therefore, the physical body, enjoyable as it is, is not a necessity to my forward moving.

I am consciousness has neither beginning nor end; it only has continuous unfoldment.

Life can only be to me what I am to it. Knowing myself as all Life, not just a fraction of It, I am set free from the delusion of beginnings and endings. Appearance and disappearance at the level of the senses does not mean beginning and ending of consciousness. It denotes the way consciousness works. The consciousness which can cause appearance and disappearance at the level of the senses uses this means as a form of self-expression. But this form is one of untold numbers of forms. The tomato I ate yesterday did not stop the creating of tomatoes next spring. To me, it was the appearance and disappearance of the tomato. To the creative process, it was the logical culmination of its creation of that particular tomato.

The human body, like the tomato, is subconscious intelligence operating as form. But you are not only subconscious intelligence; you are also conscious intelligence. Subconscious intelligence appears and disappears at the form level. Conscious consciousness is never seen, never measured, and has no form. This is what you really are. This produces form, but is never imprisoned by the form it produces. Knowing this, you are functioning at a level where death is unknown as a finality, but is observed as a part of the continuous progressive unfoldment of ideas.

Your decisions regarding the near or distant future should always have a loophole in them. They should never be final. Place no false mortgages on the great business of living. Expect the unexpected. There is nothing wrong with creative optimism. It is using Mind as Mind intended Itself to be used—that is, for the production of something better than that which has gone before. You are the individual who yet shall be. You are potential. You are not the individual of the now. You are the becoming person, and you do this by realizing that you are consciousness. The more this point is driven home, the more you will see yourself as limitless. Individuality is limitless because it is the individualization of that Cause which is forever free.

All definitions are temporary in meaning. The only power they have is that of the instant. They have this power only because of your belief. We are always redefining ourselves, thus reaffirming our limitations. A definition is a fence. It is a wall we build around a concept, thinking it to be a truth. A truth can never be defined. It can only be experienced at the level of our present consciousness. Your definition of an opera after first hearing it will be quite different from your opinion after hearing it twenty times. The spirit of God in you cannot be defined in the dictionary sense, for consciousness is always beyond definition. It is that which at the instant is. By its very nature, it can never remain the same. Nothing in your real being is constant. You as consciousness are not the same you who read the opening page of this chapter. This is not because you have agreed with the ideas presented. In fact, you may have disagreed heartily with these concepts. Your very agreement or disagreement has changed your consciousness.

Clarification

By this time, you may be asking what all this has to do with making decisions. Will it help you to select your next home? Will it help you in making decisions in your business. It most certainly will do just that. Any ideas that shift your attention from effect to cause clear consciousness. I have been explaining what I believe you to really be. You have to be more than that which you think you are. There must be more to life than paying bills, raising families, and achieving some material success.

For thousands of years, religion and philosophy have been seeking answers to the above ideas. Both systems of thought have raised up great minds to wrestle with the problems of life. Great enlightenment and enrichment have come from those men and women who sought to see mankind in a larger framework. A few of them glimpsed the individual as he is in the Infinite Order and proclaimed his possibility. Others saw man entrenched in materiality and placed their attention on his errors of omission and commission. They sought ways and means of making mankind *good.* From their theological and philosophical systems have come most of today's traditional thinking.

They state that the individual makes mistakes, or wrong decisions, because it is his basic nature to do so. With this, I cannot agree. I am certain that our basic nature is of a higher level than making wrong decisions. There is something of God in every person. I call this Individuality. Again, I return to the premise, *I am consciousness.* This is a definition of you that is beyond the frame of reference known as good and evil. It is the uncontaminated you. It is you as potential. It is not you as an accumulation of experience that includes good and evil. It is the *you* who moves through experience but is untouched by the problems and the decisions of experience.

Great spiritual thinkers have stated that the world we live in from the age of one to one hundred years is an experience world, but not a final world. Most religions declare this. I am certain this is so. Therefore, I explain my ideas that, as you enlarge your self-concept and see yourself in a larger picture, you are wiser and your decisions will be wiser. First of all, you will cease your worrying over wrong decisions. If this book does nothing more than that, it shall have a valuable reason for being written. We have wept too long over the past and what it might have been had we been wiser. This is not only useless contemplation, it is a negative one and, therefore, places further negation in the subconscious mind for it to digest and probably manifest.

Wrong Decisions

Any wrong decision you have ever made will become unimportant when your attention is shifted from it to a creative reason for living right here and now. The adult mind, proceeding with the business of living, is forced by the necessity of thinking in the *now* to forget the mistakes of childhood. You know that you cannot go forward by thinking backward. Experience has taught you a great deal, and you use the wisdom of that experience to handle the affairs at hand.

New ideas are always as near as your next thought. Mind is inexhaustible, and you are an individualization of Mind. You are an adult person in an adult world, and your thinking must be that of the adult. Every moment of your waking hours, you are making decisions. Most of these will be right; a few of them may be wrong. Over a period of time, you may discover that the decisions which you thought were wrong were actually right. Often the mist of material thinking beclouds our sense of values. Time clears our vision and we see things as they really were.

No power is sitting in judgment on any person. In the older systems of thought, we eased our guilt load by believing that God would punish us later for our errors. Now we see that this is not so. All guilt is self-guilt. There are no records being kept except in our own subconscious memory field. There is no deity to judge or punish. There is only Life proceeding, and those who can minimize their mistaken decisions proceed with Life, as Life. The larger your understanding of yourself as consciousness, the freer you are of guilt. You place your attention on bringing to pass your next right action. Your optimism is undisturbed. You have learned from your mistakes, but are not stymied by them. This is the way of progressive order, the way of creative thinking.

Goal Decisions

Man does not live by bread alone; he lives by making decisions. In my many years of counseling people, I have learned a great deal about the art and the science of making healthy decisions. Most of the people who have consulted with me were in problems. These problems were mainly the result of wrong decisions. Always they ask, "Why did I do it?" Psychology has the answer to that one, and the explanations of the psychologists are helpful. But there has to be more than an explanation of why a negative situation happened. There has to be hope. Unless I can revive a hope in these people, I cannot help them.

Hope is a spiritual potential in everyone's mind. Too many people use it as a fantasy, as a delusion, as a means of dodging the decisions that need to be made at the moment. But many times I have noted that people in trouble need to have the potential of hope revived in their consciousness, while still realizing that the decisions of the present cannot be avoided. The hope revived clears their negative considerations a bit. It lessens their questions regarding their trouble. It starts them thinking ahead with some optimism, slight though it may be. It quickens the spirit within them and lets light begin to lessen their darkness.

There has to be an expectancy of approaching good for a mind to be healthy. Tomorrow has to be interesting in order to live creatively. The depressed person does not know this. The attention is fixed upon why he or she is in the problem. The creative thinker's attention is fixed on how to get out of his problem. It might benefit the reader of this book to pause and find out which attitude is his. It is obvious that there are no final problems. There is always a solution to any situation. This is not only a platitude; it is a truth. Every remedial science and art is premised on this truth. There is always a way out. Many never find it because of their negative, defeated attitudes. Every remedial science and art has its failures as well as its successes. Many will read this book, proclaim it valuable, and profit by it not at all. Others will assimilate the ideas in it, with which they are in accord, and find them very useful in making decisions.

Mental expectancy is the key to mental health or mental depression. Behind all this is the fact of the long-range goal. Does the person have one, or doesn't he? Upon this question hinge the results that the person can have from a remedial science or art. Although I have discussed this in the previous chapters, I need to re-emphasize it from a new angle.

Some years ago, a member of my church came to me

for consultation. During the conversation, she told me of her long-range goal. It was a negative one, and most certainly an immoral one. Judging from my years of experience in counseling, it was neither a new one nor, to me, a disturbing one, for I knew it could be changed. At least she had a long-range goal. That was more than many people whom I counseled had in life. This woman knew where she wanted to go in life. I listened and did not sit in judgment. I knew that the mental process which had clarified her thought in the direction of a negative could also clarify her thought in the direction of a positive. After much discussion, this is exactly what took place in her consciousness. Her mental and emotional energies responded to the new goal with the same enthusiastic fervor that they had responded to the previous goal.

When Is *Good,* Good

Too many of the people, whom this world labels as *good,* are actually static, frightened people. They lack the courage to do wrong. This is not true goodness, as you well know. It is static consciousness maintaining the present in the hope that it is the answer. Only a mind with a creative goal is a sound mind, what I would call a *good* mind. To stand still in life and maintain the present with a battery of cliches is actually a disintegrating process. It may appear on the surface that this person is succeeding. He may be a model citizen, a devoted parent, and the epitome of character. But death is at work in his consciousness, and in rare moments, he senses that all is not well with his life.

The world has never been enriched by the standing-still people of virtue. Creative thinkers thinking progressively have wrought the procession of progress. Their goodness was not only in their morality, but in their forward-searching minds. No matter how good and comfortable the present might have been, these men and women risked discomfort to explore that which could be. This is true goodness, and it is yours if you want it. Perhaps you are too comfortable in life. All your decisions are about the everyday matters of living. You think you are secure both in the now and in the years to come. You may be the one who needs a dramatic change. The routines of comfort always resist dramatic changes. They want no new decisions to challenge the security of the moment. They have faith in their innate goodness and believe themselves to be the people worthy of heaven.

Your goal and your decisions regarding it are vital to you. Spiritual thinking is never *now* thinking. Finished ideas are not creative. Unfinished business is life. Nature is never satisfied. It is always in competition with itself. It is seeking to bring to fruition something better than that which has been before. Nature is the naturalness of God. It is Mind creating the new and the improved. All evolution is evidence of a progressive Mind thinking in new terms to bring forth improvement. This process is in you; in fact, it is what you are.

The Danger of Complacency

Complacency is an evil. It has no place in the creative process. When it enthralls your mind, subconscious trouble begins. It may be months or years before you are aware of the disintegration it has produced. You may laugh it off, but the degenerative process continues until you wake up. Eventually, some serious problem arises which stops you short and makes you re-evaluate your consciousness. Suddenly you realize that you have been drifting and not creating. You have relaxed in the false comfort of routines and paid no heed to new ideas. Your thinking and conversation are out-of-date, even though respectable. You are caught in the dying mechanism of mind. This mechanism is working this way because you have unconsciously given up living.

If anyone were to tell you that you had unconsciously given up your reason for living, you would be furious. You would point out all the values you have created in your present life. You would recount your triumphs of the past. Yet, at the center of your thought, there would be a nagging sense of failure. The feeling that all was not right. Truth would be staring you in the face. You might or might not want to see it.

Goals. The word is a taunting one to many. The aged say it is too late. The youth say they have no chance. The middle-aged state their limited aims and think they are sufficient. I dare you to think in great terms. I challenge you to dream a great dream. Nothing is impossible to those who decide upon possibility. The Infinite responds by corresponding, by becoming the thing that you have determined shall be. The framework of your preconceived opinions is the only limitation to your begetting. These are subject to change at a moment's notice when you have arrived at decision.

The following is a spiritual treatment for your use. Speak it aloud often. Ponder it. You may not agree with it, and this will be good. It will arouse new ideas in your mind. It will shake you from your mental complacency. It will quicken your resolve to arise from all mental lethargy and walk free into new vistas.

There is one God, one Mind, one Life, and one Truth. I am the beloved individualization of this creative process. There are no static situations in my life, for I renounce all static conditions in my mind. I am open and receptive to new ideas. The trap door of intuition is now open in my mind, and I am inspired by right ideas. These ideas are right for me. My goal is obvious. I now declare that all subconscious patterns in opposition to my goal are now neutralized. I know what to do and I do it. My goal is established in my consciousness as being so; therefore, it is so. I have it. I rejoice in it. I give thanks for it. It is so.

4

Decide to be Happy

HAPPINESS IS GENUINE satisfaction with your present experience. The number of people in today's world who are not happy is shocking. Think of six of your friends and estimate how many of them are satisfied with their current situations. Happiness is not a constant, but satisfaction can be. Satisfaction is a deep underlying sense of fulfillment, a sense of doing a good job with life. It is a good subconscious base which abides in certainty through the many vicissitudes at the conscious mind level of experience. It is a basic wholesomeness which permits a flow of creativity to be in action in both mind and emotions.

Unhappy people think they know why they are unhappy. The number of unhappy people I have listened to and counseled with is legion. Their explanations of the many causes of their unhappiness are usually incorrect. They do not see themselves correctly. Their disturbed emotions distort their reasoning capacity. They want to change events, situations, conditions, and people in their individual worlds. They do not want to change themselves. They want a rearrangement of facts and dodge the concept of a rearrangement of ideas within their own consciousness.

Happiness Is an Inside Job

It is obvious that, for most people in the world today, happiness is available. Everything is done that can possibly be done to make us happy. Our great corporations are producing more things for more people than ever before. They are manufacturing them faster, distributing them faster, and making them available at lower prices all the time. We exist in an almost gluttony of *things.* No longer can it be said that only people of wealth can have everything. People of lower incomes have television sets, automobiles, and good clothes. Yet unhappiness continues at all income levels and in all types of people.

If things do not make unhappy people happy, then what does? A change of consciousness is the answer, and very few people want to change their consciousness. They want to change situations in their experience while remaining in their present static states of mind. A changed experience can only happen to a changed individual. This is a mental and spiritual law. It is the truth of life, and intuitively every person knows it. Try as we may to avoid this truth, it remains true. The world responds to you by corresponding to your thought. It becomes to you what you are to it. It outpictures your consciousness and can change only when your consciousness changes. Things, situations, and events do not happen. They are caused, and your mentality is a field of causation.

Your present mind is cause to your world of effects. Everything that happens to you happens because of you.

You alone are cause to your material experience. This is perhaps a very unpleasant truth, but it has to be known and accepted if a correct way is to be found to be happy. Already in your mind are the right ideas seeking your right thinking to become cause to your inner and outer happiness. You have no need to implore the Deity. You do have need to know yourself as a great spiritual potential of happiness. God's work in you, as you, has been completely accomplished. It awaits your recognition and your practice of Its ideas. Here is a spiritual treatment to make you aware of this.

There is one Mind, God, Infinite Good. This Good includes all that I am. Therefore, It includes every idea that I need to be happy and creative. These Divine Ideas are right now functioning in my consciousness, revealing themselves to me. I am open and receptive to these Ideas. I am alert to their intuitive instruction. There is no resistance in me to my own good. There are no old patterns of unhappiness, no false ideas that I am unworthy. I am a spiritual being, an individualization of Life. My subconscious mind now accepts these statements and acts upon them. Now I know my rejoicing pathway.

It is interesting that the superabundance of things available, the ever-expanding numbers of well-educated people, and all the fields of modern science have not increased man's happiness. This does not mean we should go back to the Dark Ages and be without comforts, education, and science. It means that the world of the mind, and not the world of form, is the final arena in which to seek and to find the joy of living. The material world will make you comfortable, but it will not make you happy.

Your arrangement of your world is through the power of mind, and this you have.

Tools of the Mind

We have more techniques today to make people happy than we have ever had before. The last one hundred years have brought the birth and development of psychology, psychiatry, psychoanalysis, and our field of metaphysical science. All of these deal with mental and emotional causation. Yet, the number of unhappy people increases at a far greater rate than the facilities of psychological therapies can handle. There are not enough skilled minds to handle the increased numbers of disturbed people. That is why books of this kind are rendering a valuable service.

Whatever you need to make you happier is at hand. No longer can anyone say he is isolated. There is always something to help you, and it is where you are, if it is only the public library. Here you will find mental tools that bring light to the mind and hope to the heart. Remember, you are seeking ideas and mental attitudes to create happiness. The material world of itself cannot produce your inner sense of peace and well-being. Things cannot do it, but ideas can do it, and you are a thinker thinking ideas. So you can produce your happiness by letting creative ideas govern your everyday thinking.

The kingdom of God is within, and here is the source of ideas. Every spiritual sage has told us this. All scriptures have pointed out this truth. But we are geared in the wrong direction. We are so busy doing so many things that we fail to nurture the mind with right ideas. The consciousness of most people is starved for new, creative impulses. It is hungering and thirsting for righteousness, as the Sermon on the Mount has been proclaiming for two thousand years. This is an inside job, and we are equipped to nourish this hunger and quench this thirst by developing new ideas, finding new interests, and thinking new thoughts.

Step off the treadmill of monotonous routines and monotonous thinking. To rehash the good and the evil of the past is stupid, unnecessary and destructive. Grasp new tools of the mind for they are at hand. Great ideas are seeking your awareness. They need your mind in which to function in order to give you fuller self-expression, and your fuller self-expression brings your happiness. Frustration is sin. It is an insult to the God that created you to be a thinker. You have no need for self-hurt. You have no need for boredom. You were born to be a dynamic thinker of great ideas, producing interesting experiences for yourself and others. The equipment to do this you have by Divine Right.

Once you decide that you will be happy, you then need to state that you are now happy. This Science does not deal with the future. It deals only with the now. You may argue that you cannot state you are happy when you are unhappy; that you would be telling a lie. Actually, when you do this, you are stating a truth, for the Infinite endowed you with happiness. It is where you are and in your present mind. It is not a thing that comes and goes, nor does it have beginnings and endings. It is a spiritual constant awaiting recognition and statement. The seeming lie is preparing the way for the truth to reveal itself.

To state that you are not unhappy gives freedom to the creative ideas in your mentality to be activated, to rise out of their subconscious depths and begin their correct activity. Your negative mental states forced them into retirement for a while. Now they come out of their forced inaction and burst into creativity. On the surface, you then have intuitive insights to do something new, fresh, and different.

The Necessity of the New

Static states are not conducive to happiness. Static states produce monotony and this in turn creates boredom; and the latter was never intended for you. When you are bored, you are experiencing that which God never planned. The Infinite in Its creative process is always exciting. To be a participant in the process of the Infinite becoming variety on the plane of the finite is glorious. It is your true state. It is your normal state. It is you at your greatest and best. It is you when you are creatively happy.

Your greatest hunger is for new ideas. These new ideas that you want, need, and must have are in your mind. Declare they are there and watch them happen in you. Grasp them, use them, and rejoice in them. Then, act upon them. Do something different. Say something different. Become a different person. Try different restaurants. Change from your favorite department store. Walk down some new streets in your neighborhood, and watch for interesting things. Be a sidewalk superintendent, and watch a new building being built. Marvel at a few things for a change. All this is possible, and you can do it.

Old ideas will not create new conditions. They never have and they never will. They slow us down. It is like a gradual putting on of brakes to the mentality. Watch your mind as you balance your checkbook, and make certain that you are thinking what you want to experience. You know how much money you have in your checking account. But do you know what ideas are directing your consciousness? The latter is far more important than the former. A forward-moving consciousness is life. A static, dull consciousness is an unconscious preparation for death. Stagnating in old concepts causes your consciousness to create problems.

Problems are to the mind what pain is to the body. They are warning symbols. They are different indications that something creative must be done in the mind. Wise people know this and start reversing their thinking when the problem appears. They seek a new idea to solve it, not an old idea. It is well said that necessity is the mother of invention. You may think a minor problem is not that important, but it is. It needs your new thought about it to reduce it to nothing. Letting minor problems exist in your world means that more will be generated. Soon the aggregate of the minor problems becomes your major one. It has come to full bloom, and you are depressed.

The solution of any difficulty is as near as your next thought. All the ideas of the Infinite Mind await your claim upon them. It is a truth of the greatest importance. There is not something physical to be done; there is only a new idea to be thought. It is obvious that some form of either conscious or subconscious mental action precedes any external action. All action is dependent upon thought. As a thinker, you think thoughts and thus you have the key for controlling all the action that takes place within you, as you, and around you. Too few people know this principle and apply it. The average person lets his mind run riot and then complains bitterly about his difficulties. Tell him that he needs new ideas and to think differently than he has been thinking and he will laugh at you. The truth is that you can direct your mind and change any situation for the better. This includes your happiness. I am not saying that thinking is happiness. I am saying that thinking, based on exciting new ideas, is the cause of happiness.

When you decide to be happy, the creative process of Mind moves into instant action upon your decision. Being all-intelligent, It knows what to do and does it. Ideas reveal themselves in their purity of newness and with their endowment of total capacity to produce themselves fully in your experience. Something takes over your mind that is greater than your present mind. God moves into action in you and by means of you in order to expand the you that you know into the larger you that yet shall be. All this is done in order by means of the Law of Mind. New causes are set in motion, and new effects follow as certain as night follows day. You watch the ideas unfold. You perceive the birth process. You behold new events arising in the womb of your consciousness and emerging into your everyday life, bringing new colors, new tones, and new activities. Speak the following aloud:

The action of the Infinite Mind is the action of my mind at this instant. The Infinite never repeats Itself. It is a constant source of newness of causation. In my consciousness right now are new ideas revealing new experiences of joy. My subconscious mind now accepts these new ideas as law and brings them to pass in perfect ways. There is nothing in me to obstruct God's action. Every phase and function of my consciousness cooperates with the new ideas appearing in my thought. These new ideas, accepted by me, now make my life interesting, creative, and happy. For this, I rejoice, give thanks, and am glad.

Your Right to Happiness

Do you actually believe that you have a right to be happy? Many people do not believe this. They were raised in religious traditions that implied it was not quite decent to be happy. Especially the false religious instruction that unhappiness was a virtue, that God was nearer to the unhappy than to the glad. These negations have been implanted in the minds of millions of people. They are still being implanted by many churches. Such convictions paralyze the subconscious mind and prevent the person from knowing much happiness. Many people go from the cradle to the grave with only a few bright spots of happiness. These are tragic, embittered, and lonely souls.

In the Book of Job, we read, "the sons of God shouted for joy" (Job 38:7); and Jesus stated, "These things have I spoken unto you, that my joy might remain in you, and that your joy might be full." (John 15:11) These are but two of the many Biblical statements on the subject of joy. If you have a Bible Concordance, look up the words *joy* and *happiness.* You will be amazed to find a large number of passages in the Bible that state that joy and happiness are spiritual states that everyone should have in his day-to-day living. Old theological beliefs still have subconscious power even when the intellect has dismissed them. If you were raised in the traditional church instruction that made happiness an earthly sin, you need to do some serious thinking to reconvince your subconscious of your right to be happy and of your expectation of happiness.

There is a great need for some well-known artist to paint a picture of Jesus smiling, and another one of him laughing. I am sure that he smiled and laughed often. Great spiritual ideas are not born in gloomy minds. Gloomy, depressed minds are not the wombs of creativity. They spawn negatives, not positives. The mind of Jesus had to be a rejoicing one, for the truths that appeared by means of him are eternal verities. They have made men and women happy, and are still doing so. They lift the spirits. They console the depressed. They heal the sick. They prosper those who can accept them. They make glad the heart. Such truths came out of a rejoicing mind that knew its Source and drew upon It.

Paul wrote that we were to have that same mind in us as was in Jesus. We can, for it is already in us, awaiting our search for it. By declaring that we have this mind in us, it is activated and begins its revelation of new ideas. In turn, if accepted by us, by thinking in their terms and directions, they bring to pass improved situations that gladden both the mind and the heart. The resources for happiness, which are already within our mental grasp, are amazing. They only need to be meditated upon to be known. God has endowed us with the capacity of happiness, and this endowment is a mental one. It cannot be purchased. It has to be thought, and we are thinkers who can think ourselves into happiness. No one can keep us from such lines of thinking except ourselves. Joy is the inside of the cup, and happiness is the outside. Drink deeply of the mental draught which is life itself.

The Dangers of Boredom

A great factor in the matter of being unhappy is being bored. Many people are bored and do not even realize it. Check your mind and see if you are bored with your present situation. If so, you had better break it up and fast, for it is negative mental and emotional states that breed unhappiness. It is lazy thinking. It is thinking that is uncreative and, if indulged in too long, it becomes destructive. To be bored in today's world is nonsensical. The whole planet is exploding with interesting ideas, interesting people, and interesting events. Never before has so much music, art, and great entertainment been available. New books and interesting magazines are everywhere. Radio and television are in every home. To be bored takes a good deal of doing, and a large segment of the population is doing the doing that causes boredom.

Perhaps science has made us too comfortable. We are gadgetized people. Thinking back, I wonder how my great-grandmother ever raised a family, maintained a home, and had a healthy social life without our modern conveniences. No electric dishwashers, no modern stoves, no vacuum cleaners, no electric clothes washers, yet she lived long and well, as did the other members of her family. She was undismayed by having to pump water from a well and bring in wood for the stove. No one likes the comforts of today's living more than I do. I have great appreciation for the men and women who have invented and developed the many appliances that are in my home. Their purpose is to give us more time for creative living, and this requires of us a healthy interest in life.

Creative thinking gives a zest to living, and you are a creative thinker when you decide to be one. The feeling that it is great to be alive is a spiritual necessity. It lessens the strains and tensions of routine functioning. It quickens new ideas in consciousness, and alerts the mind to the fascinations that are available to us. It allows no morbidity, no boredom, and no lazy thinking. It prevents us from drifting in the past. It causes us to be *today* people expecting great things in our tomorrows.

Think back to the days of hand-cranked phonographs that played only one record at a time. The records could only be played a hundred times before they became scratchy and lost their clarity. Many people's minds are like the old phonograph with its records. They play the same old thinking over and over. They review the past in order to avoid the present. You hear them talk about the same old things whenever you are around them. They rethink rather than think. They are bored, but not restless. They complain but make no effort to rectify their situation. Round and round the old records go in their consciousness, spreading mental bacteria and hastening the aging process. These people look tired and old no matter what their actual ages may be.

Life is the action of the Spirit. God is never bored. The Infinite is forever Mind creating new ideas, new concepts, and new purposes. The Infinite never repeats Itself. The repetition that causes boredom is known only to man. Nature is never bored. It is always in a creative process. Even the goldfish in his globe is not bored. He keeps himself active as do canaries in their cages. They are fascinated with everything. They are Life living Itself as them. They glorify the Intelligence that created them.

We forget that we are made in the image and after the likeness of a ceaseless Creativity, an always forward-looking Mind. In our forgetfulness, we wander down the blind alleys of futility and desperation. We seem lost in our own repetitious record rerunning. If only we would pause for a moment and think a new thought, we would be back on the broad avenue of life again. We would again join the throng of creative people who love being alive at every moment and through whom great tomorrows are born. These are the sons and daughters of the eternal creation.

Check your thinking of even the past hour. It will reveal where you stand in the hallways of mind. It will either depress you or cheer you on your pathway. The latter thinking is worthy of your high calling as an individualized expression of life. Always we stand between the old that is familiar and the new that is unfamiliar. It takes courage to practice this science and to grasp the new while letting go of the old. But the end results are so satisfying. No more boredom in which to vegetate; no more complaining about everything. Instead, there is a vital interest, purposes are born, and goals are achieved.

When your relatives and close friends think of you, what kind of a person are they mentally reviewing? You are a clear-cut image in their minds. They have known you well for years. They have listened to your ideas. They have watched you under many varying circumstances. They may even know you better than you know yourself. You may say that their opinions are unimportant, that you do not care. But you should care. In their minds, you should be a creative person, an interesting person, and a valuable friend. Think about the image that other people have of you. It is an image you have created. Your actions and attitudes have formed it in the other person's consciousness. You may feel that the other party has certain prejudices and he well may have some. But, in general, the picture you have created in his mind stands as being the picture you have of yourself in your own mind. It is the projection of your own consciousness; therefore, it can always be changed when you decide to change it.

We have had enough gloom and gloomy people to take

care of civilization for the rest of time. You and I do not belong in their ranks. The fact that many important figures in every branch of the Sciences and the Arts have been unhappy and yet brought forth great creative works is to belabor the point. They could have accomplished all that they did, and probably more, if they had been happy. There is no virtue in depression, bitterness, and static living. Such states have never made anyone more spiritual, more creative, or more loving. Rather, they have emotionally crippled those who have allowed these states to become basic patterns in their subconscious minds.

I see no reason for a God to create you with a body that you can keep well, if you want to; with a mind that you can keep positive, if you want to; with emotions which will respond to your constructive attitudes; with a flexible universe around you that you can control and, in it, create good experiences—and for that God to want you to be unhappy. I am certain that each of us is equipped to be happy and destined to be happy. All negative states are self-created and can be self-neutralized.

The Chronically Unhappy

You cannot cheer up people who are chronically unhappy. You cannot make a person happy, if his subconscious pattern of happiness requires being unhappy. It is a psychological fact that many people are happy in their unhappiness, just as we know that many people are only happy when they are sick. These people can only be happy on the negative side of life. You waste your time, energy, and money trying to cheer them up. It they are close relatives, you have to endure their complaints. Realize that they are the way they are because of an unconscious need for attention. Make no attempts to reform them because you cannot reform anyone into happiness who is gaining his goal by being unhappy. Understand them and you will have better relationships with them. If they are distant relatives or friends, gradually release them out of your life. Make them Christmas-card-exchange people.

Now to the question, "Should I pray for these people?" Of course you should if they are of importance in your world. Treat that the already existing happiness mechanism in their subconscious minds is stimulated and that all their negative subconscious patterns causing their unhappiness are neutralized. Here is an example of the way to do your mental work for them.

> *God created you to be happy. In your present mind, there is the spiritual equipment to produce your well-being. This spiritual treatment now activates this subconscious mechanism. All false patterns causing your unhappiness are now neutralized and robbed of all power. Right now, wonderful new ideas born of the Infinite Spirit are in your mind, and you subconsciously accept them. They have power and authority, and they produce out of themselves new forms of good. You respond to these and rejoice in them. These are statements of Truth, and they are so.*

There are no finalities in the universe, and every person can change himself when he decides to do it. The decision to be happy starts many changes in consciousness. It reverses subconscious patterns and trends. It starts something happening. You cannot decide for the other person. He, and he alone, has to make the decision for happiness and to follow up this decision with creative ways of bringing it about. It may not be easy to accomplish this, but when he shifts his attention to positives and keeps it there, doors do open and new events take place.

The Infinite Intelligence has no destructivity in It. It has nothing in Itself to tear Itself apart. It is a harmonious whole, a unity that expresses itself as a diversity but is never changed by the diversity it has created. It is a constant positive. This is the source of your being. This is the cause of your mind and emotions. Your mind and emotions are your equipment to live life. The Infinite cannot hurt Itself, but the individual can and does. Unhappiness is a self-destructive emotional state. It is a misuse of your spiritually endowed creative equipment. The person with a fairly healthy, fairly normal mind uses this innate equipment the way it was designed to be used and moves through life with a maximum of happiness.

Attention Is Power

Where your mental attention goes, your emotions follow. This is a basic truth that any person wishing to use this Science must know. Memorize it right now. This one statement may be the very key you are seeking to change situations in your life. Mind is the only creative power, and mind is a field of interaction between thought and feeling. A wise teacher often stated that good and evil were opposite ends of the same stick. Your mind is at the center of that stick and your attention determines which way your consciousness moves. Your mental attention can be controlled. All successful people have good control of their mental attention whether or not they are consciously aware of it. They think what they want, and they want what they think.

Place your attention on the attitudes, situations, and people who will add to your well-being. Doing this is sound mental practice. It is actually affirmative prayer. It feeds into your subconscious mind the mental materials which then garner emotional equivalents to bring about the objects of your attention. It is the success process, the success mechanism. It can be used two ways. When you are worried, you are using this process destructively. This is the reverse of prayer. This is a mental and emotional movement toward the evil end of the stick. The results of such use of the mind are obvious.

Jesus suggested that we bless our enemies. I interpret this as deliberately changing my negative patterns, which I have built through this law of attention, into creative positive patterns that will produce what I really want. I take my present fears and change them into new areas of faith and expectancy of good. I take my present dislike of people and turn it into new avenues of communication where I see the best that is in everyone. I can do this when I control my attention by placing it where I want it, knowing that it starts the creative process producing what I want. All this seems so simple, but it is not. It requires self-discipline, and all effective self-discipline has to be motivated by desire. In other words, I have to really want to change. It is not a surface decision. It has to be a depth decision.

Spiritual treatment work is the shifting of your attention from a negative focus to a positive idea and holding it there long enough for it to register in the subconscious mind. This is done by taking a central statement of what you want and repeating it in various ways. This technique is fully explained in my book, *Treat Yourself to Life.** Thou-

* *Treat Yourself to Life* (Dodd, Mead and Company, New York).

sands of people have used this technique and have found that it works.

No one is happy twenty-four hours a day. But, too many are happy too few hours each day. The happier you are, the greater the basic patterns of satisfaction are being built in your subconscious. Once you have a real satisfaction pattern, you will live more easily and certainly more prosperously. Not that you will not have problems, but the problems will not get as much of your emotional attention and thus they will be more easily solved. Your mental attention stays on the level of solutions, not on the level of problems. Worry is reduced to a minimum, and faith in the goodness of mankind is expanded. You have moved from the level of fight, pressure, and argument to the level of directed attention on positives followed by intelligent right action. This is the way life was meant to be lived.

The Declaration of Independence states that every man has a right to life, liberty and the pursuit of happiness. This is a spiritual statement. It is an undeniable truth. You have this right, and you will have happiness when you pursue happiness by following the simple rules of securing it.

A Course of Action

Every major accomplishment is the result of a well-planned course of action. Such a plan puts order into the mind and the mind is unhampered by irrelevant thinking. Here is a plan I suggest you follow. I cannot guarantee results because I do not know how sincere you will be in following it. Nor do I know if you will start with enthusiasm and, a few days later, return to your old habits of worry and depression. Those who are stouthearted will get results. I know people in my congregation who came to my church after years of chronic unhappiness. I have seen some of these people change gradually into creative, positive, and happy people through the use of these ideas. Others tried and then gave up. They remained in the negatives. The ones who did change themselves are rejoicing people. They are valuable to their world, their loved ones, and to the God that created them.

It all starts with a depth decision to be happy. State aloud to yourself, *I have decided to be happy.* Do this in a firm voice for at least a week. Follow this by saying:

> *I have a right to be happy. If other people can be happy, then I can be happy. I have the same mind and emotions that they do. I now demand that my subconscious use all of its intelligence to make me happy.*

State to yourself that you believe happiness to be a spiritual gift, and that this gift is already within you. It is there by right of your being alive. The more you affirm the spiritual side of happiness and your spiritual right in having it, the sooner you will have results.

Stop all complaining. Stop telling others of your unhappiness. Find things to praise. Start seeking the good points in your relatives, friends, and co-workers. There are some good points in these people ready and waiting for you to find them. When you are asked how you feel, tell a spiritual truth though it may be a factual lie. Answer that you feel great. You never felt better. Watch your conversations, and whenever you start in with negatives, change at once to creative and interesting ideas. Your spoken word has power. Use it to produce what you want by not discussing what you do not want—and you do not want unhappiness any more. You have finished with it, and it is finishing its course with you.

Start doing new and different things. Start eating different and interesting foods. Start activating your social life. Expand your circle of friendships. Go everywhere you are invited whether or not you want to go. If you need new clothes, get them. If your home needs refreshing with wallpaper and paint, call in the decorators. Shift pictures from wall to wall. Rearrange them in various rooms.

Read more books like this one. If there is a metaphysical church in your area, attend it and support it with your money. Give a little more than you normally would in order to open up your channels of receptivity. Do not eat alone too much. Do not be alone too much. Keep in circulation with the human race. People are wonderful. God works wonders by means of people. Reactivate old hobbies or find new ones. Keep yourself well-groomed, and wear your best clothes on every possible occasion. Find things to laugh about.

You cannot do all of these things at once. Pick the ones that you can do, and get started. The most important thing to do daily is to remember that God wants you to be happy, and state this aloud. Happiness is now yours.

5

Decide to Live Richly

THE GRANDEUR OF life is known by the few when it should be known by the many. The majority of people live in part only. They are half-healthy, half-wealthy, half-happy, and half-creative. They have accepted this half way of living as normal. Once in a while, in a rare moment, they glimpse a larger life and wish that it could be so. They then return to their habitual thinking and continue to function in their halfhearted way. Half-living is abnormal and unnecessary.

You can live a much fuller life right where you are in your present circumstances. It does not require more money, a better job, a nicer home, or a different marriage partner. It requires a change of consciousness, and this you can do for you are a thinker. You are the controller of your consciousness. The moment you decide to live a richer life, your consciousness will devise the ways and means of your having it. Consciousness contains total intelligence because consciousness is the action of the Infinite Mind thinking. Your consciousness is the individualization of the total consciousness of Being. That is why it will demonstrate for you a richer life when you are certain you want it and have decided to have it.

It all depends on you, not on the world of events, things, and people. Your mind is where you live. Your world, your body, and your situation react in exact accordance to your mind. Not someone else's mind, *your* mind. An expanded consciousness expresses in an expanded experience. This is the way the law of mind works, and it works no other way. A greater and happier outward experience requires a larger and fuller knowing in consciousness to precede it.

Many people use this mental law in reverse. They think in smaller terms all the time. They unconsciously lessen their viewpoints, take less and less interest in the business of living, and wonder why they are unhappy and limited in scope. If you were to tell them that it is because of their consciousness, they would be furious. They live in the closed-in belief that nothing is their fault, that somehow the situation developed by its own causation. So they adjust to the lesser life and say that those who are able to live with ease and in order are lucky. The latter are not lucky; they are wise. They see themselves in a larger way. They not only glimpse the greater, they grasp it.

Redefine Yourself

The Psalmist wrote, "Thou openest thine hand, and satisfiest the desire of every living thing." (Psalms 145:16) This is the divine givingness in which we are forever immersed. This is why the kingdom of heaven is on earth right now and can be experienced now. The Infinite Mind, being infinite, could not create a limited creation. You are the unlimited creation of an unlimited Source that is forever giving to you Its unlimited ideas, possibilities, and potentialities. Its nature is to release Itself in you, as you. It cannot withhold Its ideas. By Its very nature, It must express Itself through man.

The Infinite is a divine extravagance. It is forever giving Itself away. God knows no thrift. The Infinite does not need to be thrifty for It is an inexhaustible mind, an inexhaustible substance. It does not need to conserve, pinch, limit, or budget. It throws Itself away for It knows that only through expression can the abundant life be lived. Expression is release, and the Infinite Mind is forever throwing Itself away, releasing Itself. In order for It to have total self-expression, It has to be a total givingness. This is the divine magnificence.

You are a part of this creative process of the Infinite throwing Itself away. You are the receiver of the infinite bounty. To you are given the total ideas of the universe. They are given to you in order that you, too, shall express them by throwing them into your subconscious with deliberate intent and thus keeping your world fresh, new, and different. All of life wants you to live fully. All the love there is wants you to love fully. All the wisdom there is wants you to know yourself aright and fully use your capacities. You have everything going rightly on your side when you understand this science and use its principles.

Oliver Wendell Holmes wrote, "Man's mind stretched to a new idea never goes back to its original dimensions." The more you are aware of the creative process and your place in it, the larger the dimensions of your consciousness and the greater your use of right decisions to keep right on expanding. The Infinite is forever thinking out, not in. God is not self-centered. God is not self-concerned, for God has nothing to fear. The Infinite knows no enemy, for there is no opposition. It has no fight, argument, or battle. It is at peace within Itself. You are the taker from the Infinite in order to be the giver to the finite.

Expression is a law of psychological health. Repression is this same law in reverse so it appears to act as a law of emotional illness. Too many religious systems have taught doctrines of repression, thereby limiting and psychologically crippling their adherents. Our system does the opposite. We know that expression is the law of Life. It is the law of Life giving Itself away by means of man. Man takes in order to give. This is the divinely balanced process of creative consciousness. When a person takes but fails to give, he has established confusion within himself and some form of deterioration begins to be born in his experience. The divine law of taking and giving cannot be abrogated without trouble being born. The following, spoken aloud, will be of help:

> *The Infinite is always imparting Itself to me. It created me in order to give Itself away by means of me. I am the divine recipient of all the ideas of Life, Truth, and Love. I now accept these ideas from the bounty which has already been given to me. My subconscious mind rejoices in this new material with its creative directives. It creates new situations better than any that have gone before. These new situations are means by which I give myself to a better world and to a finer humanity. I am the receiving and distributing process of the Divine Mind. I know myself as this. I respect myself for this. I give praise and thanks that this is so because it is so.*

Thus, you are knowing yourself as you are in God, thereby ceasing the incorrect knowledge of yourself as mere man or woman. This redefinition is essential for your health, wealth, love, and self-expression. It proclaims your wholeness to your self, that self that becomes what you declare it to be. You are whole. You are sound. You are the taking-giving action of the abundant Life. You are in your right place, doing your right work, releasing right ideas at every instant of time. You know yourself as God knows you. This clear, correct self-knowing is consciousness being used as consciousness was intended to be used. It erases the false concept of humanity for all time, revealing the true nature of divinity that has always been in your consciousness, waiting for you to know yourself as you really are by ceasing to know yourself as that which you are not.

Stretch Your Spiritual Muscles

If some of the statements made in this book seem to you to be beyond belief, even fantastic in their claims, keep on with them as they will stretch your mind a bit. This is healthy mental exercise. Most systems of physical exercise are incredible to the onlooker, yet they produce results. Persisted in, they maintain the individual in physical well-being. So will the spiritual sights that you glimpse reveal a mental and spiritual well-being if persisted in over a period of time. Many times, students in my classes have heard me repeat some of these ideas over a period of five or ten years, and then suddenly an idea clarifies itself in their minds. What to them had bordered on the absurd was suddenly a truth. Now they knew what I was teaching. Now they could benefit by this new knowledge that had suddenly burst in their consciousness.

Paul wrote, "For we know in part, and we prophesy in part. But when that which is perfect is come, then that which is in part shall be done away." (1 Corinthians 13:9-10) Spiritual truths mulled over in the mind eventually clarify themselves. Looking back at your old religious beliefs, you may wonder now how you could have ever believed them. But you did at that time believe them and would have never even read more than the first paragraph of Chapter One of this book. You would have set it aside and been rather caustic about it. To have read this far indicates that you have found some stimulating new concepts and are considering them.

A full and rich life has to be premised on spiritual understanding. As I have said before, things alone do not make a full life. They give us comfort and this in itself may lull our consciousness to sleep when spiritual ideas are suggested. For many people, spiritual ideas are incredible so they dismiss them from their thoughts. What they learned about God in childhood is equally incredible, but this they fail to realize. They have learned to live with such beliefs and see no reason for trying anything new along spiritual lines, especially when the newer ideas are garbed in strange vocabularies. New ideas have to have new vocabularies. Every new area of science, as it develops, begets new words, new phrases, and a whole new terminology. In order to present the idea of God as Mind, man as that Mind in action, and the universe as that Mind in reaction, the consciousness of the individual has to be ready to perceive words used in new ways and having new meanings.

I am thinking of all the new words and terms that have been created by the birth of the automobile. Even that word itself was created to take the place of the term, *the horseless carriage.* Every part and function of the automobile had to be given a new name. So, when you start thinking spiritually instead of theologically, you have to accept and assimilate a whole new language. Often the new terms in the new language are not really understood for a long time. Spiritual awareness expands spiritual understanding which then ennobles the whole consciousness of the individual.

New definitions and new explanations given to old spiritual terms bring enlightenment. God as Mind, instead of God as a Super-Man, opens up all kinds of questions and leads to all kinds of new thoughts and convictions. Man as a Divine Individualization of all life negates the man born to sin. All this causes mental exercise which, in turn, causes expansion in awareness. It is like living in a large city and, at dusk, watching the lights gradually come on in office buildings and homes. Everything is seen in a new dimension and, though it may not be fully comprehended, yet the mind expands.

I often say to myself, "God is wonderful. I am wonderful. Life is wonderful. All is wonderful because God is the wonder of it all." Such sentences would stick in the throats of many old-time religionists and would be considered blasphemous. I consider them to be the truth. For me, they open up new vistas, new horizons. I see myself in a larger framework. I sense the unity of all things. I have a deeper dedication to right living based upon affirmative thinking. I realize that my five-sense mind, with its great intellect, is not all there is to life. The unknown ways of the spirit can be known by me. I am not in a Spiritual Mystery that cannot be comprehended. I am in a Spiritual Explanation in which I can grow in understanding It and the ways in which It works. I do not have to take spiritual ideas on faith. I explore them until I have a clear knowledge of them. Then they are my possessions, my pearls of great price.

The full life is a field of limitless opportunity. It requires no physical labor. It bids you to think new thoughts about the eternal verities and thus reshape your conclusions. You see yourself as you have never seen yourself before. You sense the spiritual power that is really yours. A power for you to use to live richly, happily, and to give in new ways to other people. You have the sense that you are unconditioned and free. No problems control your thinking. Your thinking controls and dissipates all problems. Your knowingness is always on time. You know what you need to know at the time that you need to know it. All ideas are available to you and your mind is open and receptive to them. You rejoice in the limitless opportunity that is yours.

Those who live the full life have no fear of the future. They know that tomorrow is today amplified. Tomorrow is the outpicturing of today in a new arrangement. If there is no fear of this day, then there will be no fear in another day. Present consciousness is always the future experience. The future is secure for those who are living in mental and emotional security right now. Rather than fear the future, plan the future and put into it some excitement. It all starts with present thinking. If today's thinking is not exciting, then tomorrow's experience will not be either. As a thinker thinking, you can create what you want when you want it, and this robs the future of any negative suggestion. You are free in time. Past, present and future are controllable. The past can be cleansed. The present can be made fruitful. The future can be what you decide it shall be. All of this is possible because you are consciousness making creative decisions.

Exercising your spiritual muscles by accepting new ideas makes you aware of the wonder of it all. By knowing that all things, people, situations, and events are spiritual, you live in the amazement of the spirit. Truth, love, and beauty can be seen in everything. It is as though you suddenly saw colors for the first time. A new dimension seems to be added to everything. The pebble on the beach is not just a stone. Now it is a work of art to be studied, to be felt, to be praised. Suddenly all things great or small are of equal importance and they bring to you interesting concepts to be considered. All things add to your wealth of mind and emotion. You see where you have not seen. You feel where you have not felt. The luminosity of God pervades your whole consciousness and you know that heaven is this earth. You are in it. You are never again to be out of it. It surrounds, indwells, and fulfills itself by means of you, now that your spiritual understanding is obvious to you.

Correct Mental Achievement

The full life has no stress nor strain in it. These have been left behind to become nothing. They always were nothing, but by not knowing spiritual ideas, we made their nothingness into something we thought was real. We knowingly or unknowingly placed ourselves under their rule. Now, having accepted the full life that is ours as spiritual beings, we have declared our emancipation from these unnecessary burden-creating beliefs. Their yoke is no more upon us. We are free to move forward to achieve the desires of our hearts.

Your heart's desires are your great assets. They indicate the experiences you can have when you make your decisions to have them. They are mighty potentials awaiting your attention. They should never be ignored. With correct spiritual understanding, they can now emerge in your life to fulfill your life. As you think about them, they stir within your consciousness as the baby stirs within the mother's womb. They want out. They want to be made visible by means of you. They are knocking on the door of your intuition, trusting that you will open that door.

All creation starts with desire. God desired self-expression and the cosmos was born. The desires of your heart are the possibilities that can be manifested in your experience. Your right thinking animates them. They are restless to be born. Do not let your material, humdrum thinking keep them stifled any longer. Desires are not hopes nor are they dreams. They are potentials to be unearthed and brought to fruition. Start thinking of them as being not only possible but actually so. A few days of glimpsing their possibility will lead you into planning their arrival. Take one of them and make it so by knowing that it is so. There will be a response once you have delivered to your subconscious mind the ultimatum of your decision that this desire is to be made a fact.

Most real desires have been thwarted by indecision. People go to their deaths with unfulfilled hearts' desires because they never decided to act upon them. They were either too busy, too lazy, or too tired. Not you. Living the full life, you are busy but not too busy. You are always alert, keen and active. You have normal fatigue, but not exhausting fatigue. You can bring forth your heart's desires because now you have the tools with which to work.

To have correct mental achievement, you discard all indecision, all doubt, and all fear. You may raise the question of whether this can be done. Certainly it can be done, and you can do it. A firm decision that all indecision, doubt and fear can no longer operate in your consciousness starts their dismissal, robs them of all authority and relates them to complete unimportance. This is their death, and they can never experience a resurrection in you. You have crossed them out. Fear, indecision, and doubt may have ruled while you were in your Gethsemane of worry, but now they are crossed out in the Calvary of your decision that they are no more.

Perhaps you are one of those people who, when they use the word *God,* find a subconscious fear stirring. Do not be afraid of the word *God.* If your former religious beliefs still have subconscious power, decide that their untruths shall be revealed, and their truths shall continue to function in your consciousness. No one should fear God once God is realized as the Divine Givingness. Actually it is a wonderful word, especially when you know Its synonyms of Mind, Truth, and Love. Realizing the impersonality of the Creative Process should in itself destroy any fear of God. Say aloud to yourself:

> *I have no fear of God. The use of the word* God *cannot cause subconscious fears of a distant deity. God is where I am and what I am. The spirit of God is my spirit. The love of God is my love. The creativity of God is my creativity. I am free of all fear, for now I understand what God is. I am aware of both omnipresence and imminence. I am at ease with the words* God, Spirit, *and* Truth.

Likewise, your use of the word *God* may stir up old guilt. This is very possible. Again, it is the old false concept that God has watched every wrong thing or thought you have ever done or thought and is keeping a complete record of these which you will have to face some day. Intellectually you may know this is not so, but the subconscious mind has never been told with any definiteness that it is not so. Therefore, the old guilt about God remains. Go to work on this mentally.

A student may say to me that he now realizes that he can have what he wants in this full and rich life. He states that he has now decided on a certain objective. I reply that this is great news. He replies by saying that he is not sure that it is. Then I know that subconscious guilt is making itself apparent, that feeling of whether a personal God would approve or disapprove. His guilt is not over the objective he has decided upon; the guilt is whether God would approve. So I tell him to do specific treatment work to erase that false belief out of his subconscious mind.

Having taught this Science for a long time, I am certain that the most difficult concept for people really to accept is the one that they can have what they want in life. The old concept of the virtue of going without what you really want and accepting graciously the smaller portion of life as being a spiritual one is nonsense, and I know it. I hope by now you are convinced that you are a free agent in an impersonal creative process that responds to you by becoming the thing you desire, once you have decided to have it or to be it. If not, then go into your mental gymnasium and bat these ideas around until your subconscious mind stops acting on your old beliefs and proceeds to act upon this new belief. Then life will bring to fruition your decisions for a larger life and a greater experience.

Prosperity

In my book, *Treat Yourself to Life,* I define prosperity as the ability to do what you want to do at the instant you want to do it. This is living the full life. You will note that the goal is not money. There are as many sick rich people as there are sick poor people. There are as many unhappy rich people as there are unhappy poor people. Money is the means to an end, but it is not the end in and of itself. The belief that money will solve your problems is a delusion. It never has and it never will because your problems arise in and are created by your mind, not your checkbook. The way to solve problems is to change your thought and keep it changed. This is the correct decision to live a full life.

Prosperity is a state of consciousness which can be generated by you when you let money be a means but not an end. Money does not buy a view, though it may take you to the place where you can see it. Money does not buy love. It does not buy a mother, a father, a child, a husband, or a wife. Money does not buy the great relationships you have with close friends. Money is process, not goal. Rest assured, I am not running down the value of money. No one appreciates its uses and values more than I do. I believe it to be God in action and often state this as a truth. It is a means by which the Infinite circulates in my world of affairs giving me ease and joy. I sometimes say that money is an idea in the Mind of God, the idea of circulation and ease. Then I say that I am an idea in the Mind of God, and that these two ideas now coalesce. Therefore, I am money.

Money results from the use of ideas. Ideas produce money for they are the cause of a prosperity consciousness. Spiritual ideas are free. They cannot be copyrighted or patented. They are mine to use and I use them. I have been using them while writing this book. Spiritual ideas are always affirmative. They could never be destructive. They are thought-provoking, though at first they may seem nebulous. The thoughts they engender gradually reveal sense and then the practical aspects are obvious. You know then what to do and decide to do it. You are acting as prosperity consciousness would act.

People often tell me that they need a great deal of money right away and they are not interested in being told that they must have a prosperity consciousness. They do not want creative ideas; they want money. I realize that they will not get the money without the consciousness of money so I get out of their way. As a result of not getting the money, they say that this Science does not work. It works when you use the methods it explains to you. Everything starts in the mind and is the result of mind action. People who are always in need of immediate money need to realize that they have a bad pattern regarding money. Until they exchange it for a better pattern, their constant need will continue. Usually these people are unwise in handling money.

One of the great benefits that comes with the realization that money is God in action is that of intelligent use of money. Unrealistic debts indicate that a person has a fantasy regarding money. He thinks he can get it without either mental or physical work. This is an impossibility. The universe responds by corresponding. Integrity and sincerity are key items in a correct prosperity consciousness. To run up bills and expect some God to pay them is ridiculous. Life does not work that way. These days of easy credit have led too many people into temptation. A prosperity consciousness can only be built on the basis of sound common sense. If the way you are going to spend money or assume debt is outside the realm of common sense, you are heading for trouble. Too many people have trusted in the Lord, forgetting that the Lord helps those who help themselves. Until your subconscious habit patterns regarding money are healthy, honest, and definite, you will not prosper.

You may already have such healthy patterns. They may have been unconsciously created by your varied experiences. They may have been implanted in your subconscious mind during your younger years by your parents, or by the way in which you lived as a family. People consider these fortunate souls as being lucky, but they are not. They are at ease in their thinking about money. They automatically demonstrate ease in their worlds as a result. They may not be as clear in other areas such as health and self-expression, or they may be.

I believe there is a neurosis that accompanies serious debt. I know that in my early years, when I was just starting in the ministry and debts were seemingly necessary, I had a real sense of uneasiness that stayed with me until that day, many years later, when I owed no man. It was like a haunted feeling. It did not necessarily depress me nor hinder me from progressing in my career. Now that I am free of it, I have a much greater sense of well-being and freedom of action. I make certain my bills are paid on time. I maintain a sense of order regarding my finances. Here is one area of my life where right action prevails.

You can never escape from law and order. Those who seem to do so will find disorder increasing in their daily living. The way you handle the outer details of your life is an indication of the states of consciousness functioning in your subconscious mind. You have a right to judge a person by the way he lives, works, loves, and handles his financial responsibilities. Do some thinking about yourself. Perhaps you need to put your material world in better order. If so, start with some spiritual thinking. Think of your individual world as being in and of a spiritual law. Realize that your home, your business, your relationships with others, and your social life all take place in the Infinite Mind with Its Infinite Intelligence. This same Intelligence is in your mind. Thus you will begin seeing your world from a new viewpoint, and the ideas necessary for straightening things out will reveal themselves to you. Doing this brings a new appreciation of life and living. Strain loses its tenacious hold and serious worries cease. You have rearranged your mental patterns and have a fuller life.

Serious lack, or a fear of it, prevents you from full self-expression. You cannot be the free person you want to be. It limits your creativeness. It keeps your sights set in wrong directions. If this is your problem, right now is the time to do something about it. Make your decision that you shall be set free of all present lack and limitation, and that there shall be none in your future. It has to be a very sincere decision with deep feelings. Following that decision, make statements like these:

> *There is no rhyme nor reason for disorder in my world. My world is in God's world. God's world is governed by law and order, and so is mine. I now express the order and wisdom of the spirit. My decision to be free of all lack and all fear of lack is definite. No longer shall poverty ideas function in my subconscious mind. I now authorize my subconscious to neutralize all such habit pat-*

terns. They are no more. In their place, I now authorize healthy money patterns, healthy prosperity patterns. These new patterns are spiritual and are now in action in me. I know that this is so, and act as though it were so. I am a free, creative, prosperous individual, inspired by creative ideas that impel me to right action producing right results.

Your subconscious mind welcomes such a treatment because it is always in a state of expectancy. It is a receiving mind. By its very nature, it must act as a law of receptivity because it cannot refuse to accept what you place in it. Not being conscious, the subconscious mind has no way of knowing what you are putting in it; it only knows what to do with the material you give it. The more you watch your moods, attitudes, habits, and central ideas and stop all basic negatives from lingering in your area of attention, the richer and fuller your prosperity will be. I have known hundreds of people who have changed lifelong patterns of debt and lack by using these methods. Not quickly nor easily did the patterns change. The decision to prosper, followed by watching the conscious and subconscious minds and persisting in refusing to let negative states continue, gradually brought the light of day and a larger experience; certainly a freer experience, resulted.

Expectations

Examine your own expectations. They will tell you if you are a healthy-minded person. Our expectations are like a mental barometer. They indicate our subconscious thought patterns. They will indicate where changes need to be made. Ask yourself what do you really expect in your life at the present time. Write them down on paper. You may be startled as the days go by to see what you really are believing way down under. That subconscious mind of yours may have in it a great deal that you do not want. Healthy expectations are necessary to a healthy mind. You probably are not expecting enough out of life. You may have grown mentally dull without realizing it. You may have let minor failures and monotonous routines take over areas of your thinking. If so, the time for a change has come.

Why should you not expect the greatest and the finest in your life? We exist in a Divine Bounty that awaits our taking, and the way of taking is a mental one that starts with desire, decision, and expectancy. No one is ever too young or too old to expect great things. No one is too poor or too rich to expect great things. If you are sick, expect to get well. If you are unhappy, expect to be happy. No power outside yourself is demanding that you be miserable. All of Life wants you to be healthy, happy, and free to do what you want to do. As I write this book, I expect it to be a great book. I expect it to sell all over the world. I expect that thousands of people whom I will never meet and never know will read this book and profit by it. I know what I want to have happen, so it will happen.

Check your list of expectations quite often. They indicate just what you will get out of life at the present time. Rejoice in your good expectations and expand them. Daydream about them. Give them the food of your creative thinking. Nourish them with anticipation. Watch for all indications that they are bringing results. Jesus said, "And these signs shall follow them that believe." (Mark 16:17) Check also your expectations of doom, continued limitation, and probable failure in varying areas of your life.

Get to work on these. They are danger signals. They indicate troubles that may come to you because your subconscious mind has the materials with which to make them happen. These must be negated with authority in your mind. Do not let them linger in the halls of your mind. Use spiritual mental work to neutralize them and to create their affirmative opposites.

You may discover that you feel quite at home in your limited expectations. They have had power and authority in your mind for years. You probably did not even realize that such patterns existed in your subconscious. The sooner you take correct spiritual and mental action on these, the better. They are potentials of trouble. They are subconscious mines ready to explode, ready to rise to the surface. When they do, you may remark that the experience is just what you expected all along. The truth has become the fact. The phrase, "just what I expected would happen," is rarely used when good things happen. It is usually kept as a pronouncement of trouble. The tone that accompanies it is one of satisfaction and righteousness. The person has proven his point. He probably does not know that he has proven this entire teaching, only on the negative side. His mind has brought to him what he was subconsciously planning because of the negative materials he had placed in it. He is a negative success. His unconscious decision to have trouble has brought it to pass.

Now you know the law of mental expectation and are free to use it for a richer and fuller life. You do not have to keep on going as you have been going, unless you like the way your life is flowing. In that case, you are right in your purposes, your sense of prosperity, and your expectations. But if you want more, need more, or desire more, you now have the information you need to live fully. Others are doing it, and you might as well join in the throng of those who expect grandly.

You are a free agent as far as your mind is concerned. You alone decide what shall be. This is the responsibility of life. For one person, it opens the door to limitations and frustration. For another, it opens the wider door to freedom, growth, and true prosperity, which is the ability to do what you want to do when you want to do it. One of my favorite Bible verses is, "Both riches and honour come of thee, and thou reignest over all." (1 Chronicles 29:12) I believe that the Infinite wants every person to be free in his experience and to control it. The Spirit in you awaits your recognition and use.

6

Decide to be Healthy

FOR MORE THAN fifty years, I have been practicing spiritual mind healing. Because of my many years of practice, I am considered one of the leading authorities in this field. I know it from A to Z. The general public has always been skeptical regarding mental healing because it has never taken the pains to study the science which is its foundation. People have found it easier to scoff at it than to investigate it. They believe it is easier to use medicine or surgery than to change basic subconscious patterns of belief, and for them, this is true.

Spiritual mind healing will never be in real competition with accredited medical practice because its appeal is limited to those persons who view life as a spiritual experience. In today's successful world, they are few and far between. Faith in general has been transferred by most people from God to the checkbook. The checkbook they are certain of; as to God, they are indefinite. They may or may not believe. The checkbook guarantees them excellent medical assistance. It usually wins out.

Despite this, there are many thousands who believe in

and practice mental healing with excellent results. They are usually quiet and well-mannered and do not shout their beliefs and their healings from the roof tops nor on street corners. They are certain of what they know to be true and rely on their methods. Others combine their faith with medical assistance when the gravity of the illness deems this efficacious. There is no conflict between the systems of spiritual mind healing and medical practice in the minds of most metaphysicians today.

A hundred years ago, it was a different matter. Medicine was not progressive as it is today. The metaphysicians rejected it and denounced it. They had a total faith in mental healing, and any who did not agree with them were their enemies. They were aggressive, dynamic, and adamant. All this has changed with the tremendous strides made in the medical field. No longer can its methods be denounced. Modern medicine has earned the right to be respected. Its research programs each year reveal new and improved methods of dealing with physical and emotional illness.

I am especially interested in the emergence of psychosomatic medicine. I only wish that more expanded research could be done more quickly. Like all advances in organized medicine, the authorities are careful to make no claims, but do indicate areas of illness that seem to have psychosomatic origins and respond to psychosomatic treatment. I firmly believe that further research in this field will reveal mental-emotional causes back of a great many diseases. The pioneering psychosomaticists, Dr. Franz Alexander of Chicago and Dr. Flanders Dunbar of New York, have revealed very valuable insights into subconscious disease causation in a few areas. I am certain that further studies are being made and interesting revelations will come out of this medical field.

Health Is Normal

When we are well, we should praise our good health. Usually good health is taken for granted. One does not really think about it. The first symptom of illness sends the victim into a panic of false expectation. It is easy to realize that health is normal and sickness is abnormal. To sickness, we give great attention. To health, we give little. Knowing the power of mind as we do, this is wrong. All things respond to self-recognition, including your health.

When you do a good job of some kind, you like to be praised, to receive recognition. I am not sure but that your health and well-being would not like the same. I suggest you speak aloud the following:

There is one Source, one Cause, one Life, and one Mind. This is God. My health and well-being are this one Life functioning freely in me, as me. I praise this health. I rejoice in this health. I am this health, which is spiritual, perfect, and free. No guilt or fear in my subconscious mind can interrupt or affect this health. I declare its permanency, even as I know that the Spirit within me is permanent.

The more you impress upon your subconscious mind the normalcy and value of health, the more secure you are in your health. I am assuming that you are at the same time living in ways of health. All this will do no good if you are disobeying the obvious general routines of healthy living. Life is a science and you have to follow its laws to keep on living in health.

Authorize Your Health

I have learned from years of experience that I cannot help anyone unless he has made up his mind to be healed and believes health to be normal, and his physical problem to be unnecessary. This is the first step toward any kind of physical healing through mental and emotional means. You may think that the people seeking health through spiritual mind healing would always be this decisive. Not at all. They often come with hope, but hope is not decision. Hope is a palliative. I really think it is usually a delusion.

A person seeking health has to decide to be well before any spiritual therapy can start producing results for him. Another factor of equal importance is the expectation of being well. When a person comes to me with these two factors clearly determined in his own consciousness, I usually obtain results. The halfhearted person should use material means. The wholehearted should use metaphysics. For the latter, it will work. In the past, I have tried through counseling to induce the decision to be well in those who enter my office with halfhearted interest. I do not do this any more because it just does not work. The individual decides only because of my arguments. It still is not his decision. It is my decision rather casually accepted because he thinks I am an authority. This will not work. There are many people who cannot be helped or healed through mental means because they will not take the responsibility of making their decision for health.

The subconscious mind, which is the operative system of the body, cannot start to create a healthy body until the conscious mind acts authoritatively with a decision of health. The subconscious mind has been busy for weeks, months, or even years, gradually building a sick body. It will continue to go on maintaining these illness patterns until it receives a clear and meaningful order from the conscious mind to cease. This is why hope will not work. It carries no authority. It lacks a serious emotional impact that the subconscious must have if it is going to reverse itself.

To reverse the automatic thinking patterns in the subconscious is not an easy matter. Deep emotional impulses are in those patterns. The mechanics and the power have all been set up to go in a certain direction to produce or to maintain one result, namely sickness. To redirect patterns, with power in the exact opposite direction, to produce health takes a good amount of determination. It takes clear thinking on the part of the conscious mind. You cannot do clear thinking until a decision has been made. Then, the decision clears the mental fog, and straight thinking can follow. I am not trying to make the process of mental healing sound like hard work. I am only stating the seriousness of the decision.

Modern metaphysical healing began around the year 1860. The early teachers, who were the only researchers we had then, produced astounding healings. Dr. Phineas P. Quimby, Mrs. Mary Baker Eddy, Mrs. Emma Curtis Hopkins, Mr. and Mrs. Charles Fillmore, and Miss Nona Brooks are only a few of the many who could look any disease in the face and know it was not so. Mr. Fillmore and Miss Brooks were dear friends of mine. I often liked to get them talking about the early days of this instruction.

I vividly remember an evening in Denver, Colorado. Miss Nona Brooks, later known as Dr. Nona Brooks, had invited me to her home. (She and her two sisters had established the Divine Science College and the Divine Science Church. In the beginning, they had such remarkable healings that they were known locally as the "Healing Ladies of Denver.") When I asked her to tell me of the early days of her ministry, she told me the following story of a healing which she thought took place in 1897.

Each summer, she and her sisters vacationed in their summer home in the mountains outside of Denver. One day, a nearby farmer rushed to their house and said, "Miss Brooks, you must come right over to my house. My wife has fallen and broken her leg." She did not hesitate for a moment. She saddled her horse and rode it to the neighbor's farm, where she found the woman in great agony. She sat down at the bedside, closed her eyes, and gave the woman a spiritual mind treatment. As she treated, she heard the bones slip back into place. When she finished her treatment, the woman stated she was free of pain. Miss Brooks told the woman to get some rest, and that she would return the next day. When she arrived the next day, the woman was up and doing her usual household work. Miss Brooks said to me, "I thought nothing of this. It was what I expected."

It was what she expected. She so knew that it could be done that it never entered her mind that it could not be done. So, it was done. I asked her if she or any of her trained practitioners could do this today. Her answer was that a healing as dramatic as that one would be a rarity in today's world. The nearest doctor to that woman was thirty miles away. So Miss Brooks knew she had to be the means of healing her. Having made that decision, her thinking was straight, and her expectation that the Divine Intelligence in her patient would respond caused the healing.

People today are medically conditioned. At hand are fine doctors, ambulances, and hospitals where the finest of equipment is available. Everyone knows this. The beliefs in the mind of a person seeking medical help today are quite different from those of 1897. It takes real stamina to decide to be healthy by means of metaphysics. Thousands do make that decision, and people trained like myself are able to clear their consciousness and free their bodies of illness.

Your body always responds to your beliefs about it. This is true because your subconscious mind can only create out of your own beliefs, not out of another's beliefs. Everyone around a sick person wants him to recover, to get well. But their beliefs cannot make him well. Their well-intentioned desires have no effect upon the subconscious mind of the sick person. He alone, consciously or unconsciously, has to make the decision for health. As his subconscious has been working for some time with the emotional patterns that cause disease, it will continue in that way until a new series of intense thought patterns are injected into it to redirect the unconscious emotional process.

Often there is a weak conscious decision to be well, while at the same time there is a definite subconscious decision to be sick. The subconscious will always win out. This is true in any area of life, but is particularly true in the matter of health.

Health Is Spiritual

The Science outlined in this book is based upon a definite belief in God. Unless you have some belief in whatever you may choose to call God, you cannot be helped by this instruction. Let us face the fact that there are many people who really do not believe in God. They may think they do. They may proclaim their religious affiliation. They may even attend some church or temple occasionally. But deep down in their world of actual beliefs, they have no spiritual conviction. They accept the factual world as being true. They believe that academic science explains everything without making any attempt to find out whether or not this is true. They are busy making money, paying bills, and seeking to enjoy their experiences.

The lack of a belief in God does not seem to do these people any harm. Most of them are honest, moral, and creative. They may use a church for baptisms, weddings, and funerals but that is about all. To me, they are missing a great growth experience. Theology is not God. Many people have confused theology with God. Man is spiritual by nature, and when he has an interest in spiritual ideas, he soon discovers a great deal about himself that he has not previously known. He senses a depth support in himself, of himself. He no longer thinks he is body, emotions, and mind and that is all there is to him. He sees a reason for his being.

We are not self-caused, nor are we biological accidents of nature. We are the expression, projection, and manifestation of a larger Idea. Evolution explains the development of man, but not the causation of man. The material definition of the individual does not explain why Bach wrote great music or why Shakespeare wrote great plays. A scientific study of man's body, heredity, environment, and education does not reveal what causes a great picture to be painted or a great song to be written. Only the spirit in man can do these things. And, if the spirit is in anyone, it is in everyone. We are all vehicles of a spirit, a cause and an intelligence which is God.

God expresses in your body as life and health. Any study of body and health reveals a tremendous intelligence at work. This intelligence is a Divine Intelligence. It knows what to do when man does not know what to do. It can heal the body when It is correctly known and directed by affirmative means. It can also heal the body after surgery or other means of medical practice. I suggest you use the following to know this:

There is one Life, God, and that Life is my life now. The Mind that created my body is the Mind that maintains my body. It knows exactly what to do to keep me in good health. I affirm the perfect action of life. I praise my health for it is of God. Intelligence alerts me to every means of maintaining and expanding my health. My subconscious mind accepts these statements and acts upon them.

Spiritual recognition of your health is a great step toward any healing. It is a required premise if you are to use spiritual treatment, or affirmative prayer, as your means of restoring health. Your very recognition of this fact causes the health process to begin its perfect work. You cannot emphasize enough in your mind the fact that God is life, health, perfect action, strength, and vitality. The repetition of statements like that one causes your subconscious mind to respond by corresponding.

Stop Accepting Illness as Normal

Illness is an abnormality functioning in a bodily system that must have normalcy in order to express creative living. Sickness has a peculiar psychology of its own. It not only conditions the body, it also conditions the mind. It creates strange quirks in our consciousness. Usually it absorbs the bulk of our attention and all our decisions are made in terms of what is wrong with us. Most people seem to have a morbid fascination with the ways and means of disease. It holds them in its grasp very easily, and they do not see things rightly. It twists and changes their viewpoints.

Wives have said to me that they cannot understand their husbands' attitudes when they are sick. Husbands tell me the same thing about their wives. When sick, people become totally self-absorbed. Often they become petty tyrants and rule the entire household from their bedrooms. They lose interest in world affairs, in other people, and even in the problems of other members of their own families. They want and demand attention, and they usually get it. Many people enjoy sickness. It is a paid vacation from their jobs. The telephone is constantly ringing to find out how they are. They receive gifts of flowers, candy, and toilet water. Their mail is suddenly heavy and get-well cards arrive and are set up around the room. They are the center of everyone's attention and concern.

Sick people often trade in on their sickness. They unconsciously, or perhaps consciously, accept the good that accompanies their problems. They subconsciously want to hold on to their illness because of the many fringe benefits that accompany it. The thought of going back to work is not pleasant. The thought of having to get their own meals and wash some dishes should be avoided at all cost. They have had a subconscious need to feel important, and this need is met by the attentions they receive. The longer the illness continues, the deeper the patient wallows in self-pity while mentally creating new attention-getters.

Such people need a spiritual jolt. They have accepted their illness as normal. They pray that God will make them better while subconsciously they hope to stay ill. They really do not want to be fully well and to assume the responsibilities that accompany actual health.

You need to know God as health and health as normal. You have to decide that you are going to be well. Once you make that decision and really mean it, the spiritual forces in your mind and body go to work. Health is a *yes* system and disease is a *no* system. Life responds to affirmative thinking. It flows where the channels are open, and affirmative thinking opens the channels.

Life created you out of Itself that you might enjoy the experience of living in health and well-being. There is not now, nor has there ever been, a spiritual design for sickness. No one is ever improved spiritually by being ill. You may get rested, but you will not be improved. The Infinite Mind knows nothing of illness. It only knows Itself as health. When you start thinking as It is thinking, your recovery is certain. There is a spiritual wealth of healing power within you, waiting your affirmative call upon it. It begins its perfect work when you decide to be health and think as health would think.

Thinking Health

Unless you are severely neurotic, your mind will think about anything you want to think. You are the only thinker in your mind. Unfortunately, health for many people is not as fascinating as illness. It is difficult to define health other than as a general sense of well-being. It cannot be measured by the pulse rate, the thermometer, or the EKG.

A healthy mind is essential to maintaining a healthy body. You may not be able to think of health as *health,* but you can think of many things from a healthy viewpoint. A healthy mind is one that actually believes there is more good than evil in this world. A healthy mind believes that there are more fine people than there are mean people. A healthy mind expects right action to be taking place and, when it discovers this not to be so, is undismayed. It proceeds to correct the situation without fear or intensive worry. It is never bogged down in serious negative thinking. It is certain of itself and of its ability to handle everyday problems.

You may have this healthy mind right now. If you do not have it, you can gradually develop it. Place your attention on constructive things and people in your world and think about them. Watch them. Study them. Use your imagination so that this new way of thinking is kept vital and fascinating. Read inspirational books and magazines. Start declaring to yourself that you have a healthy mind in a healthy body, living in a healthy experience. Declare this often. You are stating a truth, and a truth that will make itself evident in you, as you. It will bear fruit after its own kind.

Watch your conversations with people. They will reveal whether you have a healthy mind or not. If you enlarge on any negative idea in your discussions, you are wrong. Minimize every negative. If it must be discussed, do it in the shortest way possible and with the least emotion. Turn then to some pleasant, creative, or affirmative subject, and start the conversation going in new directions. Here is a quote from the Bible on this point. "Whoso keepeth his mouth and his tongue keepeth his soul from troubles." (Proverbs 21:23) What you say evidences what you are. Healthy minds do not ignore negative conditions; they proceed to overcome them. There is no need to get excited over things you can do nothing about. Reserve your mental attention for creative ideas that stimulate you.

The Health Image

Use your imagination to picture yourself and all whom you know as living embodiments of health, vitality, and perfection. Your imagination is a mighty force for creating good. It is the pearl of great price among all the other great faculties of mind. It gives form and outline to ideas. It takes the concept or idea out of the realm of the nebulous and brings it into actual visualization. Making mental images of yourself as health is a vital aid to either regain health or to maintain it.

The power of your imagination is tremendous. You have watched yourself use it to magnify negatives. Now use it to expand your consciousness of well-being. Perhaps you have never really imaged yourself as vital health. Right now, think about this and start creating such an image. With your eyes closed, picture yourself as a radiant whole being. This may take a bit of doing. Put action into this picture of yourself. Health is the capacity of doing. See yourself accomplishing some goal and doing this with ease.

Also, in doing this visualization of your health, be certain not to include any present physical limitations you may have. Make the picture perfect in every way. See youthfulness, perfect sight, perfect hearing, and all other body actions and reactions as total and perfect. Do not include limitations. You are now seeing yourself as you were created to be. Erase any age conditioning. For a moment, forget yourself as you really are. You are now seeing yourself as the Infinite knows you to be. Such a picture, held in your mind for several moments, has great therapeutic power.

Your subconscious mind welcomes this new picture. Because you have consciously created it, it is a directive to your subconscious field of creative action. Doing this once or twice a day adds power to your decision to be healthy. It soon becomes a real inspiration to you and you find it simple and easy to do. Ask yourself how you would look and feel and what you would do as a total healthy individual. As your practice of this becomes habitual, it no longer enters your mind to picture yourself any other way.

In fact, such mental practice diminishes your interest in sickness of any kind. Now, if you sneeze, you do not plan on pneumonia. You realize that sneezing is a healthy way of maintaining open channels. Also, your memory of past illnesses diminishes. You find yourself totally uninterested in past health problems and you wish other people would stop telling you about theirs. Your new health picture also increases your health vocabulary. Look up the word *health* in a dictionary and then look up the meanings of all its synonyms. A few moments of doing this will provide you with some stimulating ideas.

Now you are working on the side of positives. This makes many changes in your conversations with friends and relatives. You no longer waste ten minutes discussing your own lack of vital health, and you have less patience with those who want to tell you of their symptoms. The world of health is a fascinating world. It has its own mental pictures, its own vocabulary, and its own good decisions. Now you are at home in this new world of health, and a great peace and sense of well-being is yours.

There may be times when you have to face a slight or major physical illness. But now you are spiritually equipped to meet this without fear and false speculation. You know the problem to be temporary, and your mental attitude is such that it cannot long endure. It is unwelcome in your consciousness, and you clear it out with a definite decision that it shall not be. You know that the lie is never the truth. Facing the lie of illness with the truth of health is the healing process. You picture yourself as the truth of health and you keep this picture activated in your imagination. This frees your subconscious from all fear, and it proceeds with the business of producing health for it must produce what you consistently image.

You have lost your interest in sympathy. You do not seek it from others and you find it difficult to give to others. You feel like telling the person who is ill to change his own picture of himself. You probably cannot do this as the person would resent it, so you do not yield to that temptation, even though you think it. Gradually, other people think of you as a vitally healthy person. They remark that you look healthy. Unknowingly, your radiation of health causes them to lessen their discussions of disease. When they are around you, they now talk of other things. The spirit within them is stimulated by your knowingness of health. In fact, the chronic complainers will feel uncomfortable in your presence. Your permanently decided-upon health may make some changes in your personal relationships. The chronics will gradually move out of your life and new people, who are as healthy-prone as you are, will come into your life. You will find this a healthy fellowship of kindred minds.

True Health Is Not a Fad

True health is based on the principle that God is Life, and that this Life is your life now. You did not create it, nor can you destroy it. Even when you are in the throes of illness, your health pattern remains as a spiritual pattern in your subconscious mind. It awaits your recognition and your actual decision that it shall again become operative. Sickness can never destroy health. It can only cause it to go underground and await reactivation. You cannot destroy a spiritual pattern. The Larger Mind created that pattern and individualized that pattern in you, as you. It can be ignored and even denied, but it cannot be destroyed.

Often I have told sick people about the pattern of health that they have within them. Usually they are embarrassed by this kind of talking and wish I would change the subject back to their symptoms, where they are at ease in their discussions. Once in a great while, people will listen to me and start thinking about it. They ask if this be so, why isn't their divinely created health pattern making them well. So I have to explain the principle of decision to them. They retort that they had not decided to be sick. They did not ask to be sick. They were not even thinking of being sick.

I then remind them that they also had not been planning on being well, strong, and vital and had not geared their thinking to that end. Then I look at my watch and find an excuse to get away. Occasionally, these persons will do some thinking about my ideas and, as a result, start their subconscious healing processes. The greater number are really glad that I have left the room so that now they can think the way they want to think.

Maintaining sound health is a real mental discipline. Casual thinking and an occasional pleasant thought about it is completely ineffective. Health maintenance requires consistent, definite, specific thinking to keep the whole individual consciousness at a high level. Many people are doing it daily and proving this to be a truth. They are intuitively guided to right habits for keeping their health at a high level. They follow up their right thinking with sound habits of sleep, correct eating and drinking, exercise, and recreation. They never go to extremes in anything. They are well-balanced in their routines. Crash diets and other so-called health fads they do not need. Intuitively they know what to do as well as what to think, and they do both very well. They are spiritually motivated.

God wants you to be healthy. Divine Mind created your body for that purpose and to that end. Divine Intelligence is functioning in your mind when you affirm that It is doing just that. It most certainly is functioning upon your decision to be health. You are health, not healthy. You are life, not merely alive. You are mind, not just a thinker. You are a specialized spiritual creation with the capacity to live life effectively and abundantly. You are neither a sinner nor a saint. You are a glorious means by which the Infinite acts on the plane of the finite. Say the following aloud:

I am health. I am the health of God. I am vital, strong, and creative. I rejoice in my divine inheritance of health and well-being. I praise the Mind that created me, and I think as that Mind thinks. My intuition guides me aright in all my habits of right living. I radiate this health that I am. My health is spiritually infectious to other people. I walk, talk, think, act, and love as health. I have no interest in the opposites to health. These have no place in my consciousness and no power in my experience. I am the living embodiment of the health of the Spirit.

Health Is Not Body

Health is not body. It is a state of consciousness that permeates body, but it is not the body. The body can neither make itself ill nor make itself well. The body is an impersonal, organized field of substance with no identity of its own. It has no conscious consciousness, so it does not know when it is sick or when it is well. It acts out what your consciousness is. Your heart does not know it is a heart. Your feet do not know they are feet. Your consciousness knows both the heart and the feet and acts by means of them. When you know the impersonality of the body and its functioning, you understand why your mind or consciousness determines your health.

You may think that your eating habits, drinking habits, sleeping habits, etc., make you ill or keep you well. On the surface, this would seem to be true. But these are merely the out-picturing of your consciousness. Worry is a function of consciousness and can temporarily disturb a person with excellent sleeping habits. Sudden fear is a function of consciousness and can temporarily seriously affect the digestive and elimination systems of the body.

Health is an inside job dependent upon mental health, and mental health is dependent upon right ideas and creative viewpoints. Long-standing negative emotional patterns and attitudes most certainly cause many chronic diseases.

Taking good care of your body but neglecting healthy attitudes of mind is no guarantee that you will be healthy. The action of mind is primary in all living. Philosophers have always said this. Today, modern practical metaphysics is proving it beyond the shadow of a doubt. Consciousness is what you are, and everything you experience is the result of your consciousness. Ideas are your most priceless possession. Ideas are the food of your consciousness, and your consciousness is always hungry for ideas. What you are thinking about in the sixteen hours of each day that you are awake determines what your consciousness does.

If you would select ideas to function in your mind as carefully as you select food when you are shopping, you would never be ill again. We are *ideas* people, not just *things* people. Things are the result of ideas. The idea precedes the thing. Health is an idea in the Mind of the universe. You are that Mind individualized and that same health idea is in your mind. But this health idea needs constant activation by the processes of your thinking. Depression, worry, and a sense of pressure prevent the full operation of the health idea. Such states need to be recognized and in some way dismissed.

The ideas given in this book provide ways and means of dismissing negative emotional states and replacing them with creative attitudes based on a basic faith in life. You were born to be healthy. Your consciousness was created to be a healthy mechanism for operating you in your world. It does this when the ideas fed into it are sound.

You alone determine what ideas function in your consciousness. The fact that you have free will places the responsibility for mental health right on your shoulders. You cannot dodge this fact. This is why I said earlier in this chapter that you cannot maintain consistent good health without mental and emotional discipline.

Too few are willing to keep their minds in a healthy state. Most people want to think anything they want to think and they do just that. It is no wonder that 22,800,000 people in the United States spent $350,000,000 during 1963 on medicines, drugs and doctors to cure the common cold. They thought what they wanted to think. They fed their minds with all kinds of ideas. They sought no control over resentments, jealousies, anger, hurts, or other forms of negative emotions. They were just busy living, earning, and spending. They were too busy to lift their minds to the heights where inspiration functions and where love has great healing power.

To say that these people did not know any better is to misunderstand the whole business of living. Their intuitions were trying to give them insights. The spirit of God in them was seeking to remind them of great ideas. God does not stop being God just because people are too busy with the world of things and cannot sense their intuitive urgings. They just did not really care. They hoped that the vitamins they took would do the job at the physical level that they were shirking at the mental level.

Spiritual Dependency

You can never get out of Life. Life fashioned you out of Itself, and It never ceases to be in Its creation. Its essence is intelligence and love, thought and feeling. The God that created you is the God that you can be, for all of God is in you awaiting your recognition and embodiment. Spiritual thinking is health thinking. It is God in action as you. By this, I do not mean religious, pious, or theological thinking. I mean creative thinking that permits a flow of spontaneous ideas in consciousness. The abundant life starts with great ideas in mind. Health is assured when consciousness is uncluttered by negatives of thought and feeling.

The Psalmist wrote, "for I shall yet praise him, who is the health of my countenance, and my God" (Psalms 42:11) This is sound advice to the mind that has made the decision of health. Such a mind is not afraid of the word *God.* The ways of the Spirit are ways of right thinking. Great ideas now beckon to you. Follow them into the certainty of health.

7

Decide to be Creative

AN INSPIRED MIND is a creative mind. For most people, the idea of inspiration deals only with those engaged in the creative arts. Poets, playwrights, writers, composers, and designers are expected to be inspired. The man on the street is not interested in being inspired and feels that he does not need to be. It is an unnatural word in his vocabulary. He is uneasy when he thinks about it. Without realizing it, he has set up his routines of work, home, and social activities in order to avoid inspiration. He has created mental boundaries within which he functions in seeming ease and order. He does not know it, but he is only half-living, busy though he may be.

Inspiration is a function of the Spirit, not the intellect. Being spiritual in cause, it is inherent in each person's consciousness. It is not reserved for the favored few, for there are no favored few. As I have stated before, the Divine Economy must necessitate a Divine Equality. Mind, in Its infinite capacities, is equally indwelling all consciousness. I may not know as much as another person knows, but my inspirational capacity is the same as his. It is my lifeline to creative living, and only when I am living creatively am I actually happy.

Routined living does not make for happiness. It may create efficiency, but it is an efficiency that is dull and monotonous. It lacks a spiritual verve. It may even lead to a great outer success, while at the depths of being, there is an inward failure. Living in a machine age, we tend to mechanize our minds as we do our homes and offices. We arrange our thinking patterns to bring about orderly living. We shy away from any idea that might disrupt us a bit. We have the false belief that order and efficiency give us greater ease and thus, without realizing it, we have made ease the end goal of living, which it is not.

Some years ago, a distant relative of mine came to my church only because he was visiting in New York and wanted to see how I was doing. He was really more interested in seeing how large the congregation was, and if the right people attended. In his own city, he was a member of a large church and had served in many ways in that church. The second Sunday, he did a little listening to my talk, and later in the day mentioned two ideas I had discussed from the platform. The third Sunday, he really listened. He took in the entire lecture and was intrigued by it. When he left for the airport, he remarked that he was glad he was going home. He said that, if he were to hear me speak again, he might be convinced. But, he said, he was too old now to change churches; he wanted to die in his own denomination. A few years later, he did just that. He wanted nothing to do with ideas that might cause him to do a little thinking outside of and beyond his already accepted religious beliefs.

The fact that he did not adopt my ideas did not bother me. What bothered me was to realize that the mechanics of his mind were so set in routines that any or all creative and inspiring ideas were unconsciously rejected by his consciousness. He was a successful, prosperous man, a good man by all the world's standards. I often use the scriptural phrase, "There was no room for them in the inn," (Luke 2:7), as being symbolic of the closed mind that does not want new ideas to enter it. It is the mind of self-satisfaction. Its area of curiosity is dead.

Every great spiritual teacher has warned his followers of the sin of self-satisfaction. Curiosity is a creative action of the mind. It is a necessity for creative living. No one ever knows enough, just as no one ever has enough. The present world of ideas and things is tremendous, fascinating, and explorable. It offers every individual a vast arena to explore according to his own tastes and attitudes. To be a dull person in this present world means that you have unconsciously rejected life and the curiosity that attends it.

Whatever the power may be that caused me to be on this planet at this time, I am glad that it did so. I like this present world with its challenges and its opportunities. I like most of the problems I have to meet. I handle them with some intelligence and learn greatly from them. I like living under a law of mental expansion in the creative process that is forever making new this great world of mine. I keep my curiosity alive. I do not know enough and I do not have enough. I am seeking and finding. I am knocking and the doors are opening.

We are in the Mind Inexhaustible. The Infinite never rests on Its laurels. It never stops creating for a moment. It expects us to do the same. It expects us to be fully alive, using our curiosity to feed new ideas into our consciousness. God never made a dull person. It never created an average person. It never created a satisfied person. We are a becoming people. We are a growth people. We are expanding people. We are made in the image and likeness of an Infinite Thinker forever thinking the new in an atmosphere of love or givingness. This Thinker never retreats within Itself, never ceases to be Itself. Always, Its action in us is constant, seeking expression by means of us. Knowing ourselves aright, we fulfill ourselves by being ourselves at the highest level of progressive expansion possible. Right ideas are seeds that produce a thousandfold from within themselves in our consciousness, and the resulting multiplications in turn produce the more to be accepted, assimilated, circulated, and expressed. This is the heaven process of mind, always available, always waiting for our realization of it.

The earth process of limited mental conditioning is the usual consciousness of the average person. Heaven and earth are two sides of the same Thing. Heaven is the symbol of the ever-expanding consciousness of ideas in which we are forever immersed. Earth is the symbol of our not seeing that which can be seen, of our not experiencing that which can be experienced, and of our not being that which we can be. "In earth, as it is in heaven," (Matthew 6:10), is the great truth of being. We are the means by which earth becomes heaven. We are thinkers who can direct thought. Directed thought means directed situations, events, and conditions. By directing our thought on the premise that we are in heaven, thus having the totality of consciousness as a sea in which our consciousness floats, we grasp the infinite ideas and they manifest by means of us.

The Mental Hourglass

The symbol of the hourglass comes to my mind. The upper section symbolizes the infinitude of Consciousness with all Its ideas. The lower section symbolizes the world or cosmos of form and shape, namely, material existence. Your consciousness is that filter-through point where the ideas above flow down to the world below. You are a receiver of ideas for the purpose of loosing them into form. If the filter is congested, the ideas do not flow through. They await your decongestion. All prayer and spiritual treatment is for the purpose of mental clarification, which diminishes congestion and allows heaven to appear on your earth. Spiritual mental work is not to re-think that which has been thought, but to realize that, because what has been thought was congestive in nature, it has no place in reality, no place in that Consciousness, which is God; therefore, it does not really exist at all. Only that which is spiritual exists, and lo, the flow-through is cleared and earth becomes heaven again.

This is why your consciousness is the determining factor of your experience. It lets new ideas flow through, or it rejects them because of its own congestion. Fear, worry, and other negative thinking given permission by your indecisiveness, is like silt gradually collecting in a navigable river. The day comes when it either stops navigation or it must be dredged out to clear the channel. When you are assaulted by the effects of your own thinking, you know what must be done. No external remedy will suffice. No other person or authority can do it. Delay you may, but the moment of truth arrives when you start decongesting your consciousness through correct spiritual treatment.

No wonder that Jesus said to his disciples before leaving

them, "Peace I leave with you, my peace I give unto you." (John 14:27) He wanted their consciousness not to be congested so that heaven could be on earth, so that the invisible could be made visible. Ideas stand at the filtering point of your consciousness waiting for your clarity in order to function in your consciousness and thereby appear in your world. The only obstruction is negative thought and emotion. This is all. It may take an illness, a business situation, or a family argument to make you realize this. Once you know it, you then can clear it. By knowing the truth, you can then set yourself free of the untruth. Congestion is the untruth. It is sin at the level of mind.

You are all power, all intelligence, and the potential of all right action. You can decongest the congested areas of your mind. The Source of all ideas is never congested. It has an infinite patience. It neither persuades nor punishes. It waits for the open mind through which It can flow to make heaven and earth one. Spiritual treatment removes the duality of heaven and earth and produces the unity of good, that creative way of living that should be yours at every moment. Make yours the open mind, the navigable channel for great ideas. Here is your health, your wealth, your love, and your full self-expression at no outer cost, but at an inner cost of having to give up your hurts, your errors, your negative assertions of righteousness, in order to be flexible. Yes, in order to be the individual you were designed to be from the beginning of time. Here is a spiritual mind treatment that will decongest your consciousness:

There is one Mind, God, the Source and activity of all creative ideas. This Mind is my mind now. I am one with the Mind and the heart of Being. My consciousness is Its beloved creation. In me, God thinks. In me, God feels. I am an open channel for all spiritual ideas. My consciousness welcomes them, and my subconscious mind accepts them and acts upon them. There is no mental or emotional congestion in me. Everything that would impede the flow of God's ideas through me is now denied in my consciousness. All negative states are now erased and shall act no more. I am now the means by which heaven is revealed as earth and earth is revealed as heaven. My uncongested consciousness is now replete with creative action that produces in my experience greater health, greater wealth, greater love and communication, and complete self-expression. I declare this is so. My subconscious mind accepts this treatment completely and acts upon it.

You Are Not Average

The Infinite did not create you to be an average person. Too many people, through lack of applied creativity, accept themselves as their five senses report to them the way they appear. They give up seeking the larger life that they could have, if only they realized that they were intended to have it. It is the firm conviction of this instruction that every person is a genius in some field of living, if he would only wake up to this fact and act as though it were so. You are more than what your five senses report that you are. They know nothing of the creative mind that you have. They have no way of discerning the finer points of the Spirit. They present facts, but only facts of that which is completed, never the facts of that which can be. The facts of that which can be are the creative ideas in your mind.

Go to a nearby public park and take time to really look at the trees. Not one of them is average. Each is distinct, different, and has its own personality. The Creative Power did not make one tree. Its Idea of tree, like all Its other ideas, is one of infinite variety. Each full-grown tree has total self-expression and uniqueness. It is not like any other tree. Now, think of your consciousness and ask yourself if it has any uniqueness in it. Are there any creative ideas in it? If not, then you are like an automaton. The world, your relatives, your friends, and your employer tell you what to do and you do it. They pull the strings of the puppet, and the puppet dances to their tune.

Emerson wrote, in his Essay on Self-Reliance, "Whoso would be a man, must be a non-conformist. He who would gather immortal palms must not be hindered by the name of goodness, but must explore if it be goodness. Nothing is at last sacred but the integrity of your own mind." This is clear, straight thinking that leads to a creative consciousness producing a creative life. Written more than a hundred years ago, its message is as fresh as tomorrow's breeze. No one will ever know the thousands who have awakened to creativity by absorbing those sentences alone. The integrity of your mind is dependent on your knowing what is in your mind.

Explore the areas in your present life that would come under the heading of *goodness*. If they are good, they are creative. If they are good, they deal with the here and now. If they are good, they are stimulating your mind toward greater achievements. If they are good, they are quickening your curiosity about life. If they are good, they are maintaining you in well-being. If they are good, they are inspiring you to a greater goodness.

You may discover that some areas of your present experience, which you have labeled as being good, are merely comfortable plateaus of accomplishment and you are resting. That is why Emerson told us to explore goodness in order to see if it actually is goodness, or a delusion to which we have grown accustomed. It may well be another comfortable rut in your consciousness that needs to be examined to see if there are potentials of creativity in which it can be reactivated. If not, then it should be seen for what it is and something should be done about it. It is not necessary to discard it or condemn it, but it is vital to see it as it really is.

A situation is not always good just because world opinion thinks it is good. In New Testament times, it was considered very good to know all the formal prayers and to use them on all occasions. This was expected of any man who wanted to be known in his community as a good man. Jesus exploded a spiritual bomb. He said, "And when thou prayest, thou shalt not be as the hypocrites are: for they love to pray standing in the synagogues and in the corners of the streets, that they may be seen of men." (Matthew 6:5) Then he proceeded to explain that they were to go within their own minds in quietness and find the Source of all creativity. Here is an illustration of an apparent goodness not being a real goodness. It was merely a palliative for seeming to be respectable. It was false and the wisdom in Jesus knew it. He made his followers face up to themselves.

Most of us have built psychological fortresses in our minds so as to never consider ourselves to be hypocrites. The very word brings implications with it that must be avoided like the plague. This word is not for us. We are too well-educated ever to be hypocrites. I am certain that no one is ever a hypocrite on purpose or by plan. It is a subtle acceptance that a situation is good because the world says it is good. Again, it is the easier way to live. Creative people do not live easily in their minds, though they may in their worldly comforts. They are explorers of themselves in order not to fool themselves.

Emerson might have also asked us to explore those areas we call evil or bad. These too need some searching and evaluating. The taboos handed down to us from the traditions of past centuries may need some studying in the light of today's values and needs. For centuries, divorce was considered to be a mortal sin. A divorced man or woman was considered outside the walls of good society. Finally, in the last hundred years, this old taboo has been re-examined and new, fresh viewpoints have been accepted regarding it. This is only one of the many so-called evils that could be cited.

Average people accept the good that others tell them is good. It is so because it has always been so. It is so because it is easier to accept it as so than it is to self-explore and arrive at original conclusions. The Infinite Mind is not so just because It always has been so. It is so because of Its *now* action in you, as you, which is an action of new ideas, creative ideas. God is not interested in that which is past. In the people who are aware of the Infinite as being their present source and their present true selves, average ideas have little place in their consciousness. They are alert to the actual creative good that is in their experience, and they are not impressed with those noncreative states that are still labeled as being good.

Awake Thinking

"Awake thou that sleepest, and arise from the dead." (Ephesians 5:14) Our minds are lulled to sleep with our acceptance of standards of good and evil imposed upon us by others, by tradition, or by present world standards. In Paul's letter to the Ephesians, which I have quoted above, he was writing to people who were very much alive and certainly not sleeping at the time his letter was read to them. When you are physically asleep, the functions of your body and mind are maintained by your subconscious mind. Your heartbeat, your circulation, and even your dreams are subconsciously determined. Your awake state gives you your use of your conscious mind while the subconscious mind goes right on doing its work.

The sleep people to whom Paul referred are those who do not use their conscious minds very much. They go as the world goes. They accept things as they seem to be. They question little. Alive, vital ideas do not interest these people. They prefer the dead ideas of tradition and of their own past experiences. Awakened thinking is spiritual thinking. It is using the conscious mind as it was created to be used, namely, to explore ideas and decide upon ideas. This is affirmative mental action. It is self-fulfilling mental action. It is indicative of the whole person as being in action. It is perhaps the highest use of mind by man. It is being involved in the Divine Creative Process.

Awakened minds are not seeking to retreat but to advance. They know what they want, know how to achieve it, and use methods that are right to do so. Such minds never hurt nor harm others. Such people make possible many blessings for those who are mentally asleep. They are givers, giving of the Divine Bounty of creative thought.

Their actions make obvious their progressive thinking based on the word *yes* and not on the word *no.* They only negate that which would cause them to stand still in consciousness and thereby cease their creativity. Having read this far in this book, you are probably one of these people. If so, your future will be a creative one. You will think new ideas, perceive new vistas, take on greater challenges, and drink deeply from the wells of livingness and vitality. You have shed the armor of old conclusions that safeguarded your nonoriginal thinking. You are now flexible, awake and imaginative. Your curiosity is functioning and your expectations are many, and all of them good. You are alive, not dead. You are awake, not asleep.

It is obvious that the Infinite is never asleep. The Creative Process is a twenty-four-hour-a-day process. The allegorical description of God in the opening chapters of Genesis states that God rested on the seventh day. It may be interesting as an allegorical symbol, but it most certainly is not a truth. Infinite Mind is constant in its creativeness. There is no impediment to Its action. There is no beginning and no end. There are no disruptions of Its thinking. It has been called the eternal process of *Being becoming Being.* I like to call it the Glory of God.

Awakened thinkers are not afraid of spiritual ideas. They welcome them. Being awakened thinkers, they analyze them to find their creativeness. Such people are not traditional thinkers. They respect the traditional thinking of others, but they want none of it for themselves. They may read the Bible, but they read it in terms of the present, finding meanings that are effectual right now. They do not have a God upon a distant throne. They have a God that indwells their minds as a pure cause of right ideas. They enjoy the present and have great expectations for good in the future. These people are of value to life, to God, and to mankind.

Mental Calcification

There is no quicker way to make yourself ill, miserable, or poverty-minded than to have a closed mind. It is also a sure way of alienating people, thus producing loneliness. With the loss of all possible creativity in consciousness, there comes the endless repetition of the monotonous. This is hell on earth, but most closed-minded people do not know this. They think of themselves as being in an impossible situation, so they resign themselves to it and, like martyrs, they carry their burdens. Unfortunately, these are not quiet people. They shout their grievances against life, against God, and against their fellowman.

All this is completely unnecessary. God never created a person to be a vegetable. The Infinite has endowed us all alike. A closed mind is an insult to the Mind that created you. To the open-minded, all things are possible because all ideas are available. Inspiration finds no walls created to fence it out. It activates the open-minded person and offers to him a kingdom of heaven on earth, an arena where there are no obstacles to forward-thinking. With expectancy, curiosity, inspiration, and decision, the open-minded man is invincible. His God is up-to-date. His own creative self-image is up-to-date, so his thinking is up-to-date. He is not a past-prone mind. He uses the past as a source of wisdom. He draws upon it for it has much to give him as he creates new patterns in the present. But his motivations are present ones. His creative ideas are present ones. He is open and receptive to new ideas, for in them alone is his mental health. Without them, his consciousness stagnates. Present-day living requires present-day thinking.

The calcified mind is neurotic, unhealthy, and can only create difficulties for the individual who maintains it. Its thinking is twenty years out-of-date. It is obsolete thinking seeking to recreate the past in the present and this is a metaphysical impossibility. Such thinking withers the spiritual muscles of the mind because of lack of use. The closed mind is rarely concerned with God or the things of the Spirit. It wallows within itself in a dead sea of consciousness. It needs the command of Isaiah, "Arise, shine, for thy light is come." (Isaiah 60:1) It needs a resurrection out of its current death-thinking into its true estate of life-conceiving.

Perhaps you have only a slight amount of calcified thinking. If so, now is the time to attack it, and you do this by reviewing your thinking of the past few days. The places of hardened thinking will make themselves clear to you. Realize how stupid and foolish these minor islands of concrete are. Into each one, put a new idea, the opposite of the old one. Clear out this mental rubbish before it begins to have authority. Here is a spiritual mind treatment that will give you guidelines:

The Infinite Mind knows no inflexibility. It never retreates to the past. It never destroys Itself. I am this Mind in action. My consciousness is this Mind in expression. God's Mind is up-to-date, so my consciousness is up-to-date. It is flexible. There is no calcification in it. All old ruts of thinking are now obliterated and gone. New ideas are mine. I accept them, assimilate them, circulate them, and express them. My mind is clean, fresh, and creative. God thinks in me, and I am nourished by inspiration as a result. My creativity is amazing. It renews and recreates my whole experience. I am a new person with a fresh mind, living in an interesting world. My subconscious mind accepts this treatment, and it is so right now.

Creative Side Lines

I am assuming that you have made some definite decisions since you began reading this book. Now you need the right mental atmosphere to execute them. Your subconscious mind is already working on your new decisions, creating the ways and means of their accomplishment. Praise your subconscious mind for the excellent work it is doing, even though you may not be aware, as of now, of its actions. Rest assured it is in business, working for you along the new lines you have given it. The atmosphere of praise and thanksgiving is vital in metaphysical practice. It is a mental atmosphere in which correct ideas are nourished and given their freedom to create their corresponding forms. Your subconscious mind is like the mother's womb. You have implanted in it your decision, which is a seed idea. The subconscious is now at work building a definite identity of thought that will soon emerge into your experience. Your decision is made fact by subconscious mental work. What your conscious mind is thinking while this process is going on is of vital import. A constructive, creative, and expectant attitude has to be maintained.

Doubt regarding the end result of your demonstration must not enter into your thinking. It is to be avoided at all costs. Prolonged periods of doubt can undermine all the creative work your subconscious mind is doing. Every time doubt, question, or fear begins in your mind, catch yourself and stop it. Deliberately change the way you are thinking. Force your mind to think about something interesting and pleasant. Think of relatives, friends, and coworkers who are successful, and declare that you have joined their ranks. Use your imagination to create mental images of things and events that give you pleasure. Speak aloud the Twenty-Third Psalm. Remember that what God starts, God completes. Your decision, implanted by you in your subconscious mind, was a spiritual act. Feed it with right thinking.

Are your hobbies creative and do they stir up creative thinking in you? If not, they should be discarded and new ones thought. Perhaps they have completed their cycle in your experience and need to be dropped. They may have become too comfortable and have ceased being areas of inspiration. If so, take on a new project. Be sure it is one that causes diversion from your usual routines and will give you pleasure. Do not take on a side line that you think you need for self-improvement. Such a project carries with it a strain of accomplishment. It may well be that you do not need constant self-improvement. Take a short vacation from it, and choose a hobby that is pleasant; yes, even fun.

Pleasure and fun are creative mental atmospheres. Too many people have too little pleasure in their usual week. It is a tonic that keeps the mind functioning in ways of health. There is healing power in a hearty laugh just as there is destructive power in weeping and anger. Your mind needs the pleasure idea to offset the constant work idea. The race mind has overemphasized the work idea. We all know people who have so completely accepted the work idea that they cannot accept the pleasure idea. Their jobs come first, not their mental health. They do a full day's work and take home more work for evenings and weekends. They create their own isolation and think of it as being virtuous. It is not. It is unhealthy and unwise. It is a false concept of their own importance. It is the human ego expressing. The work idea must be balanced with the pleasure idea. God did not create you to be a drone. The Infinite created you to be a valuable producer, but It also equipped you for pleasure to stimulate your creativeness.

The Infinite Mind wants you to be happy. Never forget this, and take every step necessary to ensure your happiness. It is necessary for your spiritual growth. The unhappy are spiritually declining. This is not for you. You are now on a pathway of balance between that which must be done and that which you want to do. Maintain this balance and you will maintain your creativity. When you do your work, do it well. When you have your times of pleasure, expand them to their fullness. Take from them all that you can.

Make certain your mental house is in good order. You have no further use for negative speculations. Cut them short and dismiss them. You are expecting great things of your subconscious mind. You are expecting it to give birth to the fact of your decision. This is a time to fast from all negatives. It is a time to watch especially the trends your mind is taking. Use your imagination to keep your thinking on course. It will always go in the direction you give it. You are the authority that determines your ways of thinking. Be that authority. Many times each day, check on your thinking to be certain that it is the kind of thinking that will produce for you what you want produced. Check it to see if it is sustaining the healthy mental atmosphere that your subconscious needs at this particular time. If it is not, you now know what to do. You authorize a new direction of thought. You again contemplate yourself as already having whatever it is that you have decided to have. This is not daydreaming. This is healthy thinking that guarantees results.

Keep the inspiration level in your mind high. It needs to be a constant flow through your consciousness. It is the kind of refreshment that the mind needs. It prevents you from doing what I call drab thinking. Drab thinking is unproductive thinking, and you cannot afford it at this particular time when the full action of your consciousness needs to be one of healthy expectation. Watch a growing plant for a few minutes and you will be inspired. The Intelligence at work in the plant to bring it to its present size is the same Intelligence that is functioning in you, as you. If that Intelligence has created the plant or the flower—something you cannot do—then it will create, by means of your subconscious mind, your decision into fact.

I never cease to be amazed at the Intelligence that is at work in nature. It knows exactly what to do and does it. I often declare that that same Intelligence is now operating in my consciousness. I declare that I am that Intelligence. Such statements keep the creative ideas in the mind alert as they go about their business of becoming. Inspiration can be induced in consciousness. The more you declare that you are inspired, the freer the flow of inspiration. New ideas appear to give you refreshing thought. They prevent mental staleness, which is a dead-end street. They keep a circulation of healthy thinking, which gives the mind a healthy tone.

"Strait is the gate, and narrow is the way, which leadeth unto life, and few there be that find it." (Matthew 7:14) This is directed right thinking leading to results. You have passed through the gate of decision and you are on the way of directed thinking so that the decision can become the fact. You have gone too far now to turn back. Your demonstration is certain, for you are maintaining the mental atmosphere in which it is being born. The Law of the subconscious now works mathematically without any hindrance from the conscious mind. It is free to do Its perfect work, and It is doing it. Its total know-how is in action on your idea.

Freely you have given your clear thought unto your consciousness, and freely you shall receive the result. Remember that you do not need to know how it is accomplished. You only need to know that it is already done. That which ought to be already is. I have absolute faith in the Science of the Mind and the laws that operate it. They never vary. If I do not get the results that I think I should, I do not blame the mind and its laws. I do a re-check on my thinking during the past month. Something has gone wrong in my consciousness that has given a different direction to the law of the subconscious. As a result, it turned from doing the work of thought it was doing and went off in other directions because I told it to do so.

Your mental re-check will probably tell you the reason for your not demonstrating your decision. So, you then start all over again, detemined to have the law produce what you have again decided it shall produce. In a firm voice, you speak to your own subconscious, authorizing it to produce your decision. You declare that it is already done; it is already an accomplished fact, and that this time there will be no interruptions of doubt. You then give thanks that this is so, and conclude the treatment with a loud *Amen.* The creative process of the subconscious again begins its scientific work and continues to the end result, unless you again interrupt it with confusions; but this time you will not do that.

You are a creative human being. Never forget this. You may or may not use the spiritual creativity that is your divine inheritance. That is up to you. When you do want to use it, though, you now know how to do it. You now have the tools. Start with curiosity, move then to inspiration. Then comes the moment of decision, followed by directed clear thinking. Nothing is easier to explain and, at the same time, more difficult to accomplish.

Using these mental techniques based on spiritual laws, you need never again have fears about the future. You determine your own future. You have total faith in your individual mental equipment. Never again will you bog down in the quandaries of doubts, fears, and negative speculations. Never again will you fear your fellowman nor be jealous of him. You have been set free from all that unnecessary negation. You are free to be a positive, creative person who has decided where you are going in life and uses the right-thinking method to attain your goals.

8

Decisions, Decisions, Decisions

COLUMBUS DECIDED TO cross the ocean. The American Colonies decided to become a free nation. The Wright Brothers decided to create a flying machine. Every improvement in our world has been accomplished by a decisive mind. The faltering minds, the hesitant minds, and the fearful minds have made no contributions to our ways of living. They have been followers and not leaders. They have been lifted up by other people's bootstraps. They have received but not given. They have existed, but not fully lived the life that was a free gift to them. Not having sown creative ideas into their subconscious minds, they could not reap many values in life. They have lived in the light of other people's minds. They are halfhearted, half-living, and half-dead.

Moses was inspired to take the Children of Israel out of Egypt. He decided to do it. For forty years, these people wandered through the Wilderness before entering the Promised Land. Moses' decision took them out of Egypt, but only their own decision could take them into the new country. During these forty years, a generation and a half of the older people had died. These were the stalemate people. They wanted either to stay in the Wilderness or to return to Egypt, which they still considered their real home. During this time, a new generation and a half had been born. These people had never known Egypt. They did not want to go backward. They wanted to go forward. They decided to enter the Promised Land. Their right leader, Joshua, was appointed by Moses, and under his effective, progressive thinking, they entered their new country. Their decision produced their demonstration.

Instability

"A double-minded man is unstable in all his ways." (James 1:8) He negates his real reason for being, to let ideas happen by means of him. We are here in this present life to be the vehicles of ideas. By means of us, they happen. Ideas cannot reveal themselves. They have to have people with minds conditioned to receive them. Negative ideas need negatively conditioned people. Positive ideas need creative thinkers, affirmative thinkers. Each of us receives the type of ideas according to our preconditioned consciousness. And, we have been conditioning our minds since the day we were born.

Review your general areas of thinking in the past six months and you will discover why the ideas now coming into your mind are the kind that they are. They fit into your present subconscious attitudes. If they be great and creative, rejoice. If they are not great and creative, it indicates that you need to do some attitude changing. The law of attraction in mind is foolproof. You draw unto yourself your own. Rest assured that the kind of ideas now functioning in your mind belong there because the atmosphere of your consciousness has induced their arrival and stay. A real mental housecleaning has great therapeutic value. It rids the consciousness of those attitudes, biases and hardened opinions which invite trouble. Use the techniques given in this book to do it.

You can change the directions of consciousness because you are the thinker in the consciousness. You can so think that the ideas you would like to have in your mind will appear in your mind. Think in prosperous ways and ideas will come to you that will give you greater prosperity. I have proven in my own experience that prosperity is the result of a creative mental attitude in which prospering ideas can be born. Such ideas recognized and subconsciously accepted then reveal the necessary outer things that have to be done. The double-minded man cannot prosper, for he is unable to arrive at decisions and is unable thereby to have a creative consciousness. He needs help, but his very indecisiveness prevents him from seeking it. If it is offered to him, he doubts its value.

In my years of counseling, I have found that only those who really want what they want enough to decide that they shall have it will get what they want. The others mutter at me that great statement, "with God all things are possible." (Matthew 19:26) They expect me to agree, which I do. But their concept of this statement is that it will be done unto them without any effort on their part. They expect their half-thinking to be rewarded by a whole result. This is a spiritual and mental impossibility. Those who have actually decided to have what they want do not expect special favors from the universe. They are ready and willing to think what they want long enough to get what they want. They are not afraid of the good, solid mental work of believing. They know there are no miracles.

It does take the good, solid work of believing to let the decision become the fact. The possibilities of the Infinite Mind are the possibilities of man. But we have the job of accepting one of the many possibilities, deciding upon it, and believing in a clear-cut way that it is done. God's work is to produce ideas. Man's work is to accept them and work with them in the way that I have outlined. It is the only way of success. It has been used consciously or subconsciously by every successful person. Remember that you are using the same mind that every successful individual has used or is using. All mind in all persons is equal. One may be more highly educated than another, but the mind factor is always equal. There are no large minds and small minds. All minds are alike.

It is the nature of the individual mind to accept ideas and to think about them. This is the normal business of the mind. The fairly ignorant mind and the well-educated mind are doing the same thing. They are always accepting ideas. They are always thinking about ideas. This is the action of consciousness. It always has been and it always will be. All creativity is mental action, whether it be the farmer sowing his seed or the electronic engineer pursuing his career. Both of these men have made decisions regarding ideas. There is no mental instability in either of them. Their actions are preceded by their thinking, and their thinking follows the line of their decisions. All this has nothing to do with their religious beliefs, their political beliefs, or their financial status. They are consciousness in action producing results. They are alive thinkers.

Be certain that you are an alive thinker. Watch for any indications of instability in making decisions. You may discover that in certain fields of your experience you are decisive but that in other areas you are indecisive. These latter areas need your sincere research. They indicate possible failure-prone subconscious patterns. They may even reveal unknown fears carried over from childhood. As a toothache indicates that a visit to the dentist is important, so the indecisive areas in your consciousness indicate that you need some self-examination.

Why are you indecisive in a particular area of your life? Thinking about it will reveal the subconscious reason. It may not do this at once, but eventually you will clearly know the reason. Once this is known, you will then he able to be decisive in that section of your daily living. No more wasted mental energy in that department. No more seeking advice from others regarding it. You have freed yourself from instability. You are now stabilized in decisive conclusions which accelerate your effectiveness. You have gained another area where you are in direct control and where you are the authority to your own experience. You have gained a greater self-acceptance, a greater faith in yourself. All this makes for easier living. You no longer run around in the circles of questions and doubts. You make immediate decisions and follow them with immediate right action. There is no more hesitancy on your part. You know, decide, and act.

Correct Mental Work Is Easy

The consciousness that is established in order and has definite goals does not labor with negatives and is not turned aside by unanswerable questions. It knows what it is doing to accomplish what it wants to do. It gives no attention to the many side issues that could divert it from its proper course. It holds its emotions in directed control. They support the main decision and add their power to its process of manifestation. There is no inner conflict. There is an abiding peace in the entire functioning of thought and feeling. The entire consciousness is constructive, creative and productive.

Laborious thinking indicates the need for a decision. Such thinking fatigues the mind and lessens the sharpness of the mental processes. It is thinking with resistance because there is no clear-cut desire behind it. Your own mental brakes have slowed you down, just as the brakes of an automobile slow it down. Laborious thinking can be stopped if you will do some reviewing of your desire, your goal, and your decision. Simplify your thinking down to basics. Contemplate the goal as already accomplished and you will discover a new wave of fresh thinking sweeping into your consciousness. Right ideas fall into place and fresh inspiration reveals itself. Again, you are at ease in your creative process.

"I have spoken it, I will also bring it to pass; I have purposed it, I will also do it." (Isaiah 46:11) A premise like this one makes for easy mental work. No time or energy is given to trivialities, other than those necessary for the accomplishment of the end result. The man with such a premise has no time for resentment. Most unsuccessful people have many resentments. They have unconsciously built these resentments in order to justify to themselves their lack of success. Their twisted thinking could not produce any really satisfactory situation. They are running down blind alleys of their own unconscious creation.

The success-prone person needs all his emotions creatively supporting his decision. He cannot afford negative mental-emotional diversions. He must stay on his course of constructive thinking, backed up by a healthy constructive attitude. He makes certain that his mind is not weighed down with anything which interferes with his steadfast correct thinking. To be success-prone, you need faith in yourself, faith in other people and a generally healthy mind. You need to be up-to-date in your thinking and optimistic about your future. The pessimist weighs himself down with his false expectations of disaster. He is missing the whole point of living and most certainly he is missing the real joy of being alive. He is an excellent illustration of how not to use your mind.

The mind that is uncluttered with negative emotions is the mind that can think creatively with ease. Knowing that your mind is a phase and function of the Infinite Mind helps to keep it uncluttered. The Infinite has no negative emotions. It has no hidden fears, resentments or frustrations. Its mood is always creative. Its thinking is always clear. As you affirm that Mind to be your mind, you release Its creativity as your creativity and great things happen. God is in business by means of you, and the business of God is always good and forever expanding. Say to yourself often:

My mind is forever a part of the Infinite Mind. The Infinite Mind is never disturbed. It knows no negatives. It has no fears, resentments or frustrations. Therefore, in my mind now these cannot exist and do not exist. They have no cause, continuity or conclusion. The creativity of the Infinite Mind is the creativity of my mind. The clarity of the Infinite Mind is the clarity of my mind. God is in business by means of me and the business of God is always good. Therefore, I think with ease of my accomplished goal. It is being created in my mind right now. I welcome its appearance in my experience.

Directed Thinking

Intelligent causative thinking is thinking that is goal-directed and not impeded by emotional drawbacks. I believe this to be the normal thinking of man. All else is abnormal thinking. I cannot believe that the subconscious mind was created to give man his troubles. Being born of the Infinite, its basic motivation must be that of health, happiness, love, and self-expression. Our usual use of the subconscious is really a misuse of it. It is man who has put into the subconscious mind the materials to cause him his troubles. Nothing enters your subconscious mind save by your conscious mind. If confusion is there, you have put it there. If a failure pattern is there, you have put it there. I say this not to create self-blame, but to create self-understanding.

Self-blame is quite different from self-understanding. The first is destructive and the second is constructive. All of us can search our minds and find many faults. Unless we do something to erase these, we have only added to them. We have increased our guilt load, and this lessens our capacity for originality. Our guilt loads need to be lessened, not expanded. The originality factor in too many people is wrapped in the swaddling clothes of guilt. It remains stifled and inoperative. To perceive a subconscious fault and negate it is one thing. To perceive a subconscious fault and reaffirm it is quite another thing. Using this instruction negates subconscious faults and releases originality.

Self-understanding is a sure sign of healthy thinking. You realize that you are a sum total of patterns, beliefs, and causes. The bulk of these are creative and not burdened with past mistakes. They are of the here and the now, supported by the creativity of the past. They are today's patterns, beliefs, and causes. You are at ease mentally with them. They inspire rather than conspire. They deal with apparent impediments without fear or doubt. They back up your mental planning and help execute your orders. They are your coworkers in all that you are doing. They make you feel that you are a harmonious whole.

The negative patterns you allow to continue in your subconscious mind form a conspiracy against you. They are out to get you and often they do. Their ways of operations are intelligent. They are the causes of your many forms of ills. They obstruct the creative process. They may not be able to stop the process, but they can slow it down. They do not want you to be successful, healthy, or happy. The sooner they are self-seen by you and negated, the better. There are no impediments to the success of any person save those which have been subconsciously accepted by the person. That they can be located, observed, and negated by you is the great hope of your mental-emotional life.

Have no fear of the negative patterns you may uncover in your mind. They are ready to be known and dismissed. The only fight they have in themselves is the fear you give to them. Their continuity in you needs your fears and your worried thought. If they do not receive such nourishment, they wither into minor importance. A strong demand on your part that they vacate your mind will cause their impotence. They become inactivated, and they will stay inactive for the rest of your life, unless you unconsciously reactivate them. This we all tend to do when we are in a depressed state. We think backwards.

Directed thinking can be either negative or positive. Consistent worry is directed thinking. A constant fear of the future is directed thinking. Frustrated thinking is certainly directed thinking. Such thinking must be avoided at all costs, and the only cost there is to do this is redirection of your attention to a positive goal. The person who cannot stop worrying is the person who wants to worry. He is getting some hidden or obvious benefit from it. He may be seeking sympathy and attention. You do not give sympathy to a success person; you give him praise. He has nothing in his mental make-up to warrant sympathy.

The success person is a self-made person. The failure person is also a self-made person. Both have used the materials they have placed in their subconscious minds to get them to the place where they are. One is not lucky and the other unlucky. Neither one can state that his accomplishments are the result of heredity or environment. There are as many failures among the rich as there are among the poor. Success or failure cannot be explained by anything other than the use and misuse of mental processes. The subconscious mind produces what we place in it. It is a creative process. It is a law of action.

It is axiomatic that we are the subconscious mind in action. It determines every phase of our lives. It determines our health, our relationships with others, our financial positions and our own sense of worthiness and well-being. There is no sense in blaming it for our faults nor in praising it for our virtues. Both faults and virtues are created by our own minds in accordance with the decisions we have made regarding our own lives. Given creative direction, the subconscious mind will respond to our decisions and do its normal work and create what we want. Given noncreative directions, it again does its normal work and creates troubles for us. Its impersonality cannot be overemphasized.

Successful people like what they are doing. They actually love what they are doing. Creative ideas unfold rapidly in this mental atmosphere of love and reveal their full potentials. This love invokes their inner enthusiasm. It is a source of mental vitality. The romanticists say that love rules the world, but it does not. Ideas rule the world. When ideas are positive and are given freedom to unfold in a mind that loves what it is doing, then they do rule the world of such an individual. Such directed thinking cannot be defeated by person, place, or situation. It always is victorious and successful.

Great Ideas Need You

Ideas need you. They will be born by means of someone somewhere, so it might just as well be you. The universe needs these new ideas to maintain its evolution. Life in you needs these ideas in order to have full self-expression. You need these ideas in order to feel fulfilled. They are already in your consciousness. Do some contemplative thinking, and give your intuition a chance to tell you something. Rest assured that what it will tell you will be good. It will be an idea that will enrich you in some way. It will make you a greater person. It will probably solve any important problem you may have at the moment.

If the idea is a great one, it may startle you. You may feel inadequate to grasp it and give it embodiment. That idea would not have come into your mind if you were not the right person in the right place at the right time for it to be born. Your present state of consciousness has attracted that idea. It needs that idea right now in order to stay fresh and creative. It is probably time that you had a great new idea. You need the idea as much as the idea needs you. Do not turn it aside. Examine it. Ponder it. Think of all creative ways in which you can make it happen.

We unconsciously often reject startling ideas. They seem too big for us. Their acceptance would make too many changes in our lives. Or, we really do not want to do the work which they entail. For these and many other reasons, we say *no* to them. To accept them is to give ourselves mental health. They will stir us up. They will disintegrate our complacency. They will lead us in new directions. They will bring with them new thoughts, new things, new people, and new situations. This is exactly what we need all the time. We need to be mentally jolted by a new idea. It is mental shock therapy.

The unconscious resistance to change, which many people have, is not an indication of mental health. Routines ensnare us too easily without our realizing it. To be alert and receptive to a new idea is indicative of a success-producing mind. Ideals without ideas have no virtue. The complacent mind may have lofty ideals, but it remains a nonproductive mind. Ideals are a great incentive only when the ideas that accompany them are put to practical uses. Then complacency departs and correct mental activity begins.

It has always interested me that unhappy people have no real curiosity about themselves. The full attention of their minds is on the supposed cause of their trouble. I use the word *supposed* because a psychological study of their anguish usually uncovers a cause different from the one they have been announcing. When I have a problem of any kind, I am curious as to the subconscious causes of it in me. Long ago, I gave up blaming external events and people for my troubles. I know this Science of the Mind too well to ever again do that. I begin reviewing all emotional events of the past several months, for here I will find the cause of my problem. At times, I can perceive my answer right away. Other times, it may take a week or more of occasional reviewing. But, every time, I do eventually locate the emotional cause of my trouble in my subconscious, and I then clear it.

Most self-curiosity is negative; therefore, it is avoided as much as possible. When I review emotional experiences to find the causes of my troubles, I do not consider this process a negative one, for I am seeking that which, if found and negated, will give me my cure. I consider it a technique of healing. I am seeking a negative to destroy it, not to wallow in it and thereby increase its effectiveness. To me, this is a healthy use of curiosity. Something needs to be uprooted in my subconscious and I find it and then make certain that it functions no more.

Being the center and the circumference of my experience, I accept the responsibility for all causation. Not all people are ready or willing to do this. They do not want to look in the mirror and face and handle what they see. When you can honestly accept your mind and emotions as the only real causes of your experiences, you have set yourself free of all the delusions of which the human mind is capable. Now you are on solid ground. Now you are ready to find out why the you that you are is not the you that you can be.

The you that you can be is the spiritual you that you always have been, but not until now did you know this. This true you is the you that needs and finds great ideas. The you that the Infinite created has been waiting for your recognition of yourself as it. It is like the baby chicken in the eggshell waiting for the first crack in the shell to find its real existence. Correct self-curiosity causes the shell of your fixed human opinions to crack so that the real self can appear in your consciousness and grasp creative ideas.

In this new-found freedom of being the you that is the real you is the only security there really is. It is like coming out of a crowded room into the open and taking a deep breath of fresh air. Now you know that never again will you be victimized by your own wrong decisions and the negative thinking that accompanied them. Your mind is open to all right ideas. You no longer have any receptivity to ideas you do not want to experience. The responsibilities of everyday living are no longer burdensome nor dull. Each hour is filled with accomplishment accompanied with pleasure.

Unexpected Dividends

Your decision to be yourself pays off in rich dividends. The word *impossible* is deleted from your vocabulary. It no longer has meaning. In its place now is the word *unexpected.* You are ready for that which is yet to be, knowing that all ideas concerning it are already in your mind and will appear on time and in order. You expect the unexpected and you welcome it as it appears in your consciousness and in your world. You expect health for you have no fear of illness. You know that there is nothing in your consciousness to cause illness. All mental and emotional conflicts have left forevermore.

You expect your prosperity to be completely normal and continuous. You have decided that this shall be so.

There is no longer anything in your consciousness to cause restriction. The flowing in of money is always balanced with the flowing out of money. You have a right to live graciously and you do so. All your bills are paid the day you receive them. You discover that paying bills is a pleasant experience. Your inner wisdom, born of the Spirit, guides you in all your financial matters.

You expect to be happy, for now you realize that happiness is your normal creative state of living. You are neither ashamed of being happy nor afraid of being happy. You rejoice in being alive, doing what you are doing, and feeling as you are feeling. There is nothing in your subconscious mind to make you other than happy. You have decided that this is so, and the everyday events of your life indicate that it is so. You are even glad to have problems for now you know that each one of them is soluble through your own right thinking, right deciding, and the correct use of your imagination. You are happy.

You decide to give and receive love. You know you can do this and make intelligent plans to do it. You are no longer fighting the human race. You have taken your place in it as a loving, kind and generous person. You attract to yourself people and situations which are the right ones for you. Your well-balanced emotions plus your new creative drives and interests draw to you like-minded individuals with whom you have ease of communication. There is an interchange of ideas, attitudes, and interest. Love in you finds love in them. Love in them finds love in you. The Infinite is loving by means of you, and you give It full freedom of action. No more loneliness. No more apartness. You like the feeling of being one with many people. You enrich and are enriched by your associations. You catch a glimpse of the Spirit in all whom you contact.

You have severed all connections with frustration. The dynamics of the creative ideas in your mind are now having full self-expression. This penetrates every area of your living. You are a dynamic person. People think of you as a dynamic person. You do what you want to do. You rejoice in the free flow of creative thinking which keeps your mind centered on your decided goals. You watch new ideas happen in your mind and new events take place in your experience. You are outgoing, fulfilled, and free to express yourself.

You have faith in Life. You sense yourself to be the instrument of a mighty Mind. You are convinced of the many values of living in the here and the now. Your good is not postponed or delayed. Your mind senses the spiritual activities within it and cooperates fully with them. You trust the great creative law of the subconscious mind. Your authorizations in it are left free to produce themselves. You are free of all deep concern and serious worry. You know that only the good is on your pathway and that its revelations to you will always be the right ones at the right time appearing in order. You are affirmative in your attitudes. You like yourself as you are, creative and victorious.

You have a larger understanding of God. Not my God, nor a God of creeds, but the God your own thinking has discovered within you. It is a God personal to you, for you personalize It. You trust the Infinite Mind as It functions in your mind. You know that Its constant flow of new ideas is your guarantee of right living, for you now are receptive to them. You find many people who think of God as you think of God. You are no longer rejecting anything spiritual. You are open and receptive to spiritual ideas. You know that your life is the life of God. You know you are the living representative of all that the Infinite is. You are worthy of your high calling as a spiritual creation.

Trust in Life

There is no reason for not feeling comfortable in this great cosmos. People with self-conditioned limited minds may fear the unknown, but there is no reason for you to do this. You know that anything and everything that you need to know you will know when you need to know it. You do not need to know the future or fear the future, for you are creating your future with your present attitude. A trust in the general business of life is essential to well-being. It comes from seeing yourself correctly. You are not a biological accident. You are a programmed individual, individualizing the magnificence of Life. Any feeling of your inferiority or insignificance is ridiculous.

You are important to Life. That which created you and brought you this far will take care of you for the rest of eternity. You are a citizen of the universe, and no claim that you can make is too much for the Power which is within you to accomplish. It knows no limitations, not even the ones you have placed within your own thinking. Give this Power great works to do by maintaining great ideas in your consciousness. The creative process of your subconscious mind is inexhaustible. It knows neither worry nor fatigue. It is perfect in its precision. Give it great goals to accomplish. Use it for greatness.

When you trust the creative power of the universe, you know what real relaxation is. You do not have to solve the problems of the world unless you are the head of a government. You do not have to solve other people's troubles unless you are a professional counselor. You do have to solve your own problems, and this you do without fuss and anxiety. You make right decisions and let the subconscious mind do the work. Your attitude is, "I am resolved what to do." (Luke 16:4) Therefore, tensions regarding decisions cannot arise in your mind, emotions and body.

To trust in Life reduces the pressures of everyday living. It makes you feel that the whole world is supporting you at all times. This is exactly what the world is doing. Something great, wonderful, and true is backing up each of us. Knowing this, there is almost nothing to fear, not even death. You are a continuum. Your consciousness does not stop when your heart stops beating. You are an individual in Infinity and Eternity. You go right on living in a different environment. A fear of death is understandable in an ignorant mind, but not in yours. You are life that goes right on living, evolving, and being.

Bodies die, not people. You are not your body; you are an individual using a body. You have had many bodies during your lifetime. You started with a newborn baby's body about six to eight pounds in weight. Six years later, you had a different body. At fourteen, you had another type body; at thirty, you had another. Your present body is temporary, as were the ones you have used all through your years of living. You, as consciousness, moved through these bodies. You, as consciousness, will continue to flow through bodies; not visible to your family and friends, but very visible to you. When you state that a dear friend just died, you are talking of his or her body only. Consciousness cannot die.

I cannot believe that an Intelligence that created me out of Itself, and gave me the tools to use for creative living where I am, has no further use for me or plans for me.

Most of us are not really valuable to life until we are past fifty. Many people are at their most creative peak when their bodies cease functioning. No, you and I have a great deal of vital living to do in the millions of years ahead of us. There is no heaven and there is no hell, but there are creative areas in this ever-expanding universe where we keep on being ourselves. God will still be in business a thousand years from now and we are God's business.

Summing It Up

I have written about fifty thousand words on this science of decision. You have read them. No book can ever be a final authority. The final authority is only in the individual mind and its opinions which lead to decisions. You are an active intelligence functioning in a universe of intelligence that always responds to you as you present yourself to it. You are more than a human mind managing to get through seventy or ninety human years. You are more than family, job, home, and recreation. You are a creator creating creation. You are an infinite possibility. You will never know the full greatness that you are.

As you think of yourself in larger terms, you invite larger ideas into your consciousness. Your decisions regarding these ideas are the way life becomes to you. Individuality means independence. Independence means the necessity for assuming self-authority. You were not born to be like other people. You are a unique representation of an Infinite Source. You are always free to fail or to succeed. Nothing is predestined.

To change long-standing negative habit patterns in the subconscious mind is not easy, but it can be done and you can do it. The valley of indecision and the mountaintops of decision are both available to you. By taking authority over your own mind and emotions, you can have great mountaintop experiences. You leave behind you the valley with its shadows. You leave behind you half-living. You have assumed the responsibility of being the light to your own world. You know that you can achieve what you want to achieve. You know that all life responds to you as an infinite givingness and fills full the cup you give to it. The size of the cup *you* determine.

Your subconscious mind is a divine instrument. Its dexterity and precision will never be fully known. It is the greatest gift that you have. It is beyond price. It is what you are as a creative individual. It accepts the impress of your thought and acts upon it. It knows neither good nor evil yet its processes can create both. Wise men have said that all creation is the result of the Law and the Word. The subconscious is the Law. What you place in it is the Word. This is the play of life upon itself.

A correct definition of a spiritually acclimated individual is one whose conscious mind, operating in a field of subconscious creative intelligence, gives it creative decisions which it then produces as experience. For such a man or woman, there is a full life. They are not only fulfilled themselves; they are also able to give greatly to others. Of them can be said, "He hath done all things well." (Mark 7:37) You are invited to join their ranks and have all the benefits that accompany right decisions.

WHAT MIND CAN CONCEIVE
MAN CAN ACHIEVE